Freedom From America

for safeguarding democracy & the economic & cultural integrity
of peoples

1987 pages
_2006_

SMEs

Robert Corfe is a prolific writer who has written extensively
on the benefits of social capitalism. He is a political scientist
and businessman, with considerable experience of political
life, and in this book he sets out the arguments for a
worldwide systematic anti-Americanism, as the only means
for reviving effective democracy. For many years he was a
senior manager in manufacturing industry, and later a
management consultant advising SMEs, usually in the
engineering sector. He is also the author of two
autobiographical books under different pseudonyms: **Death
in Riyadh** _dark secrets in hidden Arabia_ (Geoff Carter),
based on his experiences as a businessman in the Middle
East in the 1980s, and, **My Conflict with a Soviet Spy** _the
story of the Ron Evans spy case_ (Eddie Miller), based on his
adventures in Scandinavia in the 1960s. In 1987 he founded
the Campaign For Industry, to which he was elected
Chairman, and for which he wrote many pamphlets on the
problems of contemporary business. His broad experience,
frequent travels overseas, and years of residence in
Continental Europe have given him a unique perspective of
socio-economic issues.

Freedom
From America

for safeguarding democracy & the economic & cultural integrity of peoples

Robert Corfe

Arena Books

First published in 2006 by Arena Books
Second impression

Arena Books
6 Southgate Green
Bury St. Edmunds
IP33 2BL

Corfe, Robert
   Freedom From America for safeguarding democracy &
   the economic & cultural integrity of peoples
   1. United States – Civilization – 1945- 2. United States -
   Foreign relations – 21st century 3. United States - Foreign
   Relations – 20th century 4. United States – Politics and
   Government – 1989- 5. United States – Politics and
   Government – 1945 - 1989
   I. Title
   973.9'3

ISBN 0-9543161-5-0

Printed & bound by Rowland Phototypesetting Ltd.,
Bury St. Edmunds, IP32 6NU.

Cover design
By Jon Baxter

Typeset in
Times New Roman

PREFACE

Anti-Americanism as a political concept has not merely become a topic for discussion, or an option to be weighed pro or contra, but an imperative for the sanity and stability of the world. America is the oppressor of peoples and nations, rich and poor, across the globe. There are many justifications for anti-Americanism, but there is one which rises above all others: viz., a financial-industrial system, or a particular form of capitalism, which clashes with the long traditions of the social democracies in Europe and the Far East.

Two incompatible capitalist systems have emerged most noticeably amongst the advanced industrial economies in the post-War period: Neo-American capitalism (the label used by the French economist, Michel Albert), or what for many years I have preferred to give the more descriptive title of Rentier capitalism; versus the Rhine mode of capitalism (Albert's label) to include the Far East Tigers, or what I have always described as Productive capitalism. The two systems are represented by their own ideologies: the Neo-Liberalism of America and the Social Democracy of Europe and the Far East.

The term "Liberalism" in Neo-Liberalism refers to the call for free markets, and nothing more than this. The term is somewhat hypocritical, for whilst the emphasis is addressed to the outside world to open up its markets to American financial penetration, that country also remains the most protectionist in the world. The more accurate term, but less commonly used for obvious sensitivity reasons, is Neo-Conservatism.

Meanwhile, the term Social Democracy does not refer to a political party in this sense, but rather to a set of political beliefs accepted across the parliamentary spectrum of many different nation states. Hence the social democratic consensus refers to the existence of the welfare state; workers' and trades' union rights; and the need for the state to oversee (but not necessarily operate) effective financial support for the sick, the unemployed, and those in old age, etc., as accepted and promoted by parties of both left and right.

As we all know, this long-standing and successful system, which has brought social and economic stability and peace of mind to so many millions in many countries is now breaking down. The fiction has been created that the social democratic consensus is now unworkable, and that in the wake of this, we must change our ideas as to how we manage our future. The real truth, however, is that the might of American corporate power through the instrument of Rentier capitalism, and guided by the belief system of Neo-Liberalism, is simply worming its way into the diverse financial-industrial networks of the world, and buying its way into the ownership of the planet. The blatant power lust or greed which this entails is in great part disguised by the fact that much of this activity is undertaken through nominally transnational or faceless institutions which cannot always be associated with any one nation.

But such a deceptive situation is soon belied by the changing appearance of the high street, not merely in the EU but throughout the world. As the pattern of private family-sized businesses disappear throughout the non-American world, it is American chains and supermarkets which increasingly take their place. If we turn to the pattern of businesses on industrial estates, be it service or manufacturing industry, the situation is worse. An initial survey of signs and logos may momentarily convey an impression of thriving private businesses, but once the pattern of ownership is investigated (as I have experienced in my capacity in management consultancy) a very different picture emerges. What at first appears to be an estate of private business, is soon revealed to be in the ownership of groups, and those groups in the ownership of corporations with their power base in Chicago, New York or Detroit.

Now the pattern of international ownership within a state need not in itself be a cause for alarm, but if such penetration is undertaken by a country with quite another ideology, then a very different situation emerges. And this is the situation with America. Neo-Liberalism represents a historical tradition in sharp contrast to the economies of the non-American world. The free-wheeling, pioneering, double-crossing, cow-boy spirit, not only evokes a business culture very different from that of Europe or the Far East, but more significantly, entails a perspective of life, society, and their aspirations very different from that of other peoples.

Just as non-Americans may dislike what they see in the land of the dollar, then Americans may equally dislike what they see in lands beyond their own frontiers. Whilst the non-American world recognises the need of the state to take some measures in protecting its citizens from the hazards of illness, unemployment, poverty, or old age, the American is dismissive towards any idea of a safety-net, which he condemns as patronising, demeaning to the individual, and "Socialistic." So deeply-seated is the American aversion to the idea of the benevolent state, that the very thought of it fills him with shame.

With the fall of the Berlin Wall and the collapse of the East bloc in 1989, America unexpectedly found herself in a position of unprecedented power. As soon as she recovered her balance, and realised the significance of the new political power pattern, she seized the opportunity which was open. Before the world had time to realise the truth, the intelligentsia of America took the initiative by reminding the establishment that their country was now unchallengeable, and that Neo-Liberalism was destined to conquer the world. In the forefront of such a campaign, and in smoothing the path for the great corporations, was the need to discredit the financial-industrial systems or the capitalism of Europe and the Far East.

Until the fall of the Berlin Wall, America had been circumspect in her relationship with the rest of the advanced industrialised world with regard to its very different financial-industrial systems and modes of funding business. She retained sufficient discretion not to criticise the principles of deficit financing, or the magnificent role which the industrial investment credit institutions had played so successfully throughout Japan, Western Europe, and elsewhere in the decades after 1945. But with the fall of the Berlin Wall the gloves were off, and America embarked on a clever war of attrition against the traditional financial systems of the other advanced industrial economies. She did this because they cramped the style and frustrated the methods of the American corporations in their bid for an ever larger slice of the economic cake.

It was against this onslaught that the Frenchman, Michel Albert, tentatively produced his book, *Capitalism Against Capitalism* in 1991. It was launched as a warning to the economies of Continental Europe against the evils of Reagan-Thatcherite economics and the disastrous social consequences that this would bring to ordinary people from Finland down to Portugal, or from the Netherlands to Greece. Albert put emphasis on the economic factors, but in refraining to cause offence, or too great a controversy, he chose to play down the political aspects. The present author, who came to similar conclusions, and published his views in two pamphlets six years earlier,[1] had no compunction in being forthright in the outcome of his research or professional experience.

Since then much has occurred. Using Britain as a launching pad, American business has penetrated every part of Europe – both East and West – as well as many other territories throughout the world. It should be noted that whilst Britain is historically the sole fully developed Rentier capitalist economy in Europe, her tradition of social welfare and protection policies places her politically within the social democratic camp of the Continent and the Far East Tiger economies.

Why is it so necessary to resist American economic power, even when disguised within the bland framework of international corporations? Because when subjected to close analysis the outcome of Rentier capitalism is anti-democratic and anti-social. The feeding of smaller fish to larger creates an ever-decreasing ownership class, as franchises and corporations turn former proprietors and managing directors into powerless functionaries working to a given formula, or into a salariat

---

[1] These were, *New Life For British Industry*, and, *An Open Letter To The Manufacturers of Britain*, both published by Centre Publications in September 1985.

answerable to the financial control of a distant authority. So-called "owners," or managers, or chief executives, are transformed into eunuchs, and become dependent on the decisions of others. They are never *ultimate decision-makers* and because of this they are poor material as participants within the life of their communities.

If they contribute to the community it is not as free agents but as the mouthpiece of their controlling corporations; and as they are dependent on a superior for their livelihood, they can never be trusted in their judgement as contributors to the democratic life of the community. Governmental democracy arose through the basis of personal property qualifications, and although today we may be appalled how this restricted the franchise, it did have the value of connecting the individual to the business and needs of the community in which he lived. And now all that is gone, a class of the powerless, the uncommitted or the "bought," are expected to participate meaningfully within our democratic life.

Rentier capitalism gives rise to many other ills in society: it polarises wealth between rich and poor; it leads to poverty, injustice, and high crime rates; it leads to financial instability and exacerbates the problems of cyclical downturns; it undermines commercially viable productivity through the need to maintain price levels, and share and dividend values; it finds the restraining demands of environmentalism an intolerable burden on its activities; and lastly, it is self-destructive through the need to grant ever-higher levels of personal credit in maintaining the demands of consumerism. All these facts have been made evident again and again, especially when comparisons are made between the social conditions of societies existing under Productive or Rentier economies. These are the reasons why we must fight to maintain Productive capitalism, Social Wealth Creation, and the social democratic consensus; and fight against the Rentier capitalism of America, Unsocial Wealth Creation, and Neo-Liberalism.

Resulting from the evils of American commercial power are the more visible ills which may be summarised under the heading of the undermining of the cultural integrity of nation states. Every country has the right and duty to its people and traditions to uphold its cultural integrity against the encroachment of a foreign power. This includes the right to its own language; religious beliefs; customs, manners, and modes of thinking; the arts and cultural mindset. Of course there has to be free cultural interaction and exchange between all nation states – and this has always existed – but we are not referring here to such a situation.

We are now concerned with a single mighty power, with little respect and much disdain for all cultures foreign to itself, swamping the world with its own artefacts and particular view of life and society. And this is the great wrong which is being inflicted on the world. It is a great wrong not only because, as we argue in this book, that American values are false and anti-democratic, and against the needs of humankind by any objective psychological or ethical criteria, but because the unwarranted cultural domination of any nation state is unjustifiably invasive and so objectionable.

In addition to the above, there are other factors of even greater significance that now make anti-Americanism a political imperative by peoples of goodwill throughout the world. Throughout the advanced industrialised economies of Europe and the Far East, and further afield, democratic political systems are breaking down. This is made evident by the collapse of party memberships of all parliamentary groups across the political spectrum, as well as by declining turnout figures of voters during election periods.

This is because the underlying class-based thought patterns of parliamentary groups are trapped in a time-warp of the past, and have not been able to keep abreast with the reality of social and technological change over the past two generations. Although responsible centre left parties attempt to eschew class-based politics by appealing to every sector of the community, in the public eye they have *not* been able to overcome their ideological legacy of promoting a class-based politics. Today we live in a heterogeneous society of the middle-middle majority, which is multi-class, and essentially tolerant to majorities and minorities alike. It is only intolerant and disdainful of the intolerant, and this includes an intolerance of politics which draws its support through the apparent discrimination of class.

There are huge numbers of working class people, especially in the private and industrial sectors, who are repelled by what they perceive as "wrong-headed" or "mischievous" attempts to arouse discontent in the workplace; in the same way that there are many in the middle and upper classes with a strong social conscience who are repelled by the politics of the right. Higher educational and skill levels throughout every sector of society, contributing to a greater equalising of educational chances have helped to militate against a class-based view of addressing political issues.

The above situation is compounded by the fact that the major issues of today do not easily lend themselves to a class-based approach. Environmental issues are an obvious example of this, but economic questions arising from our financial-industrial institutions, i.e. industrial investment, financial services, pensions, etc., impact equally on every sector of society in different ways. It is true that at the present time in Britain, for example, there is an increasing polarisation at either end of the social spectrum between rich and poor, but the 90% majority are nonetheless inextricably bound and made dependent in some way on a life-long basis within the embrace of the financial system.

If we turn to the problems arising from globalisation, e.g., the increased volatility of market forces, de-industrialisation, off-shoring, out-sourcing, etc., the situation is even more dramatic with regard to the magnitude of economic threats which equally effect those across the spectrum of society, and render them impotent to effect political change. The real and worsening problems now confronting us can only be addressed as complex technical issues, and if they are to be intelligently resolved, it cannot be through the confusing prism of a class-based perspective.

This creates an exceptionally difficult situation for political and democratic life. If questions cannot be resolved democratically through the conventional means of representation, then how can they be resolved? Many would instinctively reply that there is no other alternative. Issues could be resolved through the representation of functional groups, or through a sophisticated system of referenda, but this still leaves open another problem in the sphere of practical politics.

Democracy or any representative system, or indeed, the advance of political life by any other means in pushing forward the demands of society, cannot be achieved without the motivating force of anger or resentment against wrongdoing, howsoever this is defined. Anger is the essential dynamic without which it is impossible to imagine that politics could survive. It is the realisation of this fact which keeps in existence the established pattern of confrontational politics, but for want of any alternative, it is only kept alive as a kind of living death. The present pattern of politics frustrates and distorts the resolution of issues at every stage during which they are addressed.

What is the way out of this seemingly impossible maze? There is an answer to the difficulty, and it is so obvious, it confronts us on an almost daily basis. As with many of the most insuperable problems in society, the answer lies at our feet. It is the need for anti-Americanism! This is because all the major political issues facing the world today are traceable directly to the malign power of America. It is the power of America which enforces an undesirable system of capitalism on the peoples of the world, and it is America which is the major power responsible for resisting a response to global warming and cutting back on the exhaustion of fossil fuels.

Anti-Americanism launched and pursued as a political ideology would therefore succeed in concentrating on the core problems confronting today's world in a way that no other approach could hope to rival. If the critique of the American financial-industrial system was confined to how it operates within the States, the discussion would cover issues sufficiently distant from the non-American world to be considered with objectivity and candour. This is because the critique would not be *directly* threatening to individuals or systems elsewhere, except as a consequence of invasive politico-economic forces. This would therefore allow for what we might therefore describe as a politically *scientific* anti-Americanism, i.e. an anti-Americanism not so much based on subjective feelings as on disinterested fact.

The major problems which face us today, irrespective of whether they be environmental or economic, are not national but *international*. They are international because the power of governments are unable to overcome them. The contemporary pattern of representative politics is futile and impotent in the face of these problems. Existing democratic struggle compounds rather than resolves the thorniest issues of our time, and that is the reason for the apathy and disillusion with *party* politics throughout the advanced industrialised world. It is also the reason calling for the necessity of a systematic anti-Americanism. In confronting effectively the massive problems of the future, we need to muster the support of 90% majorities and not merely the 50% majorities of the conventional politics of the past. And that is why and how the cause of anti-Americanism will aid the revival of positive democracy throughout the globe.

In this Preface we have hardly touched on the disastrous record of America's consistent failure in the international sphere, particularly in the field of ideologically-driven warfare in territories across the globe. Now war is a costly business! We live in a world where we must choose between "butter or guns." When small countries are inveigled by the most powerful country on earth to join them in bombing and occupying chosen targets, their governments may be flattered by the invitation to share in the glory.

But in due course, it also means their peoples' must pay the penalty. The payback may be hidden, but when pensions are slashed; when jobs are lost due to declining investment; when markets fall; when public services are cut; when free health at the point of need becomes an "economic liability;" and when poverty is on the increase, it is not the time to ask the reason why. The old politics, of course, in its sheer stupidity, may raise its ugly head in casting misdirected blame, but it will not offer an ounce of commonsense in resolving the real issues.

It is at America where the finger should be pointed, and it is through the call of anti-Americanism that democracy will be revived. This is because the origin of all conflictual problems must be tracked down to their original source if democracy is to be based on reality and not illusion. The confrontational process, being the essence of democracy, must aim its shaft at the real evils in our midst and not at phantoms, if it is to succeed in advancing humanity towards a better future. And as it is America which generates the political ills of our world, it is in the manifestation of that power where all political struggle should be concentrated in the future.

Anti-Americanism as a worldwide phenomenon is not recent in its origins. It has been varied and deep-seated amongst most peoples and across all sectors of society for a long period of time, but in this book and for the first time, we attempt to present a rationale to justify anti-Americanism on both ethical and political grounds, and to demonstrate how her population are uniquely different from all other peoples.

This does not mean we have presented a critique of the intrinsic humanity of Americans as individuals, although on the rare occasion, in our indignation, the rude remark may have slipped through, but we have criticised their underlying culture, which we believe is the origin of everything we dislike about America and its influence on the world. In the final analysis, however, we conclude on a note of hope, in that the American people will themselves resolve the problem of their country by opting for socio-economic change. And when that eventuality is realised, all humankind may achieve a lasting unity and concord.

Robert Corfe
January 2006

CONTENTS

CONTENTS

CHAPTER 3
America and the Debasement of Cultural Values

CONTENTS

CHAPTER I

AMERICA VERSUS THE WORLD

"North American civilisation is one of the ugliest to have emerged in human history, and it has engulfed the world."

Arthur Charles Erickson, *Speech at Simon Fraser University*, 1973.

1 – Defining the great divide

The mental attitude of the American mindset is distinct from that of any other people or race on earth in a way that no other peoples or races are distinct from one another. This, therefore, marks a clear separation in the cultural-political understanding between Americans and the rest of humanity.

Whilst the identification of such a divide may be taken as a call for anti-Americanism in the collective sense, it is not intended as a call for anti-Americanism applied to the individual. As G.K. Chesterton has so nicely expressed it, "There is nothing the matter with Americans except their ideals. The real American is all right; it is only the ideal American who is all wrong."[2]

And neither is it suggested that Americans have not produced valued bodies of specialised learning and research, or that there are not many amongst their number of goodwill and moral worth. And neither is it a call for demonising their political or industrial leaders, who rather should be pitied for their intellectual limitations, their errors of judgement, and their inability to apply ethical criteria to practical decision-making. It might also be noted that the author of this book does not belong to that toffee-nosed tight-lipped type of Englishman instinctively loathed by so many Americans. This is possibly because he is plain speaking and ill-endowed with the qualities of self-

---

[2] G.K. Chesterton, *New York Times*, 1st February 1931.

effacement, and consequently, he has mixed successfully with Americans, in both business and social milieus, usually gaining their adherence and respect.

Despite these reservations, the fact remains that it is the collective will of a people which leaves its greater mark on the wider world, and the more powerful the nation state, so all the greater may be the weight of its oppression. America has now become an aggressive and tyrannical force throughout the four corners of the globe, oppressing industrially advanced and developing countries alike, and the time has now arrived for forming a great international bond of peoples against the world bully.

2 – An end to the old bases for conflict

Left/right politics as a constructive divide in resolving the issues of the day is now everywhere breaking down. Now in the 21st century, the ideologies with which they were associated are discredited, and leave no impact on the minds of modern men and women.

This has resulted from two causes: firstly, the transformation of society over the past 60 years, and the creation of a great classless heterogeneous middle-middle majority which abhors the concept of social discrimination or conflict under any guise; and secondly, because greater problems now confront society in total, and these are not easily adapted as class-based issues.

These emerging problems concern threats to the planet, i.e. climate change, the erosion of the ozone layer, and the excessive burning of fossil fuels, etc., or senseless wars of aggression which bring benefit to none except arms manufacturers; or the dominating power of transnational enterprises, and downsizing and outsourcing, which follow in their wake.

These are ills which are present now, and accelerating, and affect us all. The chief executive of the industrial plant and his senior managers have nothing less to lose than their shop-floor workers; and office and IT employees, or those in call centres are now losing their jobs as frequently as those engaged in manufacturing tangibles.

These emerging problems cut across the entire spectrum of society and make nonsense of the politics of the past. The left/right divide has become meaningless to all – except to that small minority of discredited politicians with a vested interest in linking their salaries to the pursuit of stale and bankrupt ideas. To the majority, the left/right conflict has no more validity in the resolution of problems than the old wars of religion; and when it is not regarded as a great electioneering pretence, it is considered as empty mischief-making.

For all these reasons, therefore, in the causes of civilisation, justice, and equity, those politicians who attempt to ingratiate themselves with America must be discredited and exposed to the just ridicule which they deserve.

3 – The internationalisation of political issues

In today's world, therefore, what kind of political vision and resulting practice makes sense, or can hope to be effective? Today's politics is international as never before. Nation states and peoples within the framework of democracies have never been as powerless or as impotent as they are today.

Transnational corporations and global money markets rule as forces unaccountable to any authority. They are responsible to no one and democratically accountable to none. The financial power of governments in exerting the will of elected majorities has been reduced to a farce – and if it has not become a fraud, it has become a great pretence. Meanwhile, private investors have never had a greater reason to fear the future.

The only resource for people to change the future are democratic mechanisms, but if these are to be effective four conditions are necessary: firstly, the issues must be alive in capturing the imagination and passion of majorities; secondly, they must be obvious and concrete in their appeal; thirdly, they must reflect a *real* clash of interests between economic power groups of comparable strength and size; and fourthly, there must be the will for efficient organisation.

Hence, the politics of the future must be international in scope, and if it is to confront *significant* as opposed to *nominal* issues, it must challenge directly the power of finance rather than vainly seeking out political groups for opposition on principle. This is because the greater ills in society do not originate within political parties *per se* – and neither should they be perceived as such – but rather from impersonal socio-economic forces.

And because of this, it makes greater sense to launch a *direct* attack on such forces rather than on the usually skewed or inaccurate perceptions of political groups which serve rather as a feint in diverting blows away from the real ills to be confronted. This assertion is further supported by the fact that the general public *learn little or nothing of significance* about the mechanistic failures of financial-industrial systems from the lips of politicians, usually because of the ignorance of the latter.

4 – America is the enemy of world justice

The politics of the future, in serving the international needs of justice and equity, points the accusing finger, inescapably, at America, as the source of all political power, confusion, and injustice in the world today. To turn a blind eye to the reality of that fact, and its malign influence throughout the four corners of the globe, would amount to relinquishing all democratic rights or effective attempts at political change for peoples worldwide.

No other source of underlying social conflict exists today, for all significant politico-economic power is traceable back to America. To deny the reality of this is to retreat into an impotent politics of illusion and fantasy which rests on the dead theory of the past.

What precisely defines the malign influence of American power? It is to be found in the theory and practice of corporate power, defining the investor as the sole rationale for business activity, with the inevitable macro-economic outcome of the polarisation of wealth through the continuing accumulation of smaller enterprises by larger.

This leads to the ever-increasing dispossession of property in both the business and domestic spheres of life; to increasing personal debt to the banks; and finally, to the absorption of the political establishment and the puppet-like manipulation of the representative party system. At that point, democracy becomes a dead letter, or is maintained as empty form.

5 – The ideology of corporate power

The ideology of corporate power is promoted through the *newspeak* term of *privatisation*. This term was launched effectively during the Cold War period in contrasting it with *public ownership* or the *nationalisation* of discredited old-style Socialism. But privatisation is highly deceptive in its economic or political usage, for in reality it has no connection with anything which is "private" if understood as meaning "personal."

Instead, privatisation means the powerful organisation of corporations which are hardly less touchable or amenable to change by the ordinary citizen than the state-run bodies of an old Socialist regime.[3] Corporate power in America is no less total in exerting its muscle than was statist power in Soviet Russia. Corporate America may be a lesser evil *to its own people* than was statist power in Soviet Russia, but it nonetheless remains an overwhelming ill both within and outside the north American continent.

6 – Benign and malign economic systems

This calls, therefore, for a challenge to American power and everything she represents. But what pivotal idea could hope to make such a challenge a viable practicality? Unless there is a constructive idea – the formulation of some positive and

---

[3] The "private" or smaller investor is, of course, a part owner of the corporation, and whilst in theory may flatter his vanity because of this, in practice his influence is negligible.

practical system – nothing can be achieved, and no intelligent challenge can be made. No long-lasting political challenge can be made unless it is based on rational and objective criteria transcending the prejudice of mere "dislike."

Fortunately, there is not far to look. The post-War system of capitalism as found throughout Continental Western Europe, as well as amongst the Far East Tigers on the other side of the globe, based on deficit financing (or bank borrowing) as contrasted with the equity investing of corporations, illustrate the existence of two contrasting financial-industrial systems.

The European and Far East modes of business, so successful in building productive industry in conjunction with maintaining the social democratic consensus, and denominated the *Productive economy* or *Productive capitalism*, contrasts sharply with the American system of *Rentier capitalism*. Each system is not only driven by a different rationale: Rentier capitalism for maximising shareholders' profits, and Productive capitalism for maximising market share and long-term efficiency; but the first polarises wealth between rich and poor, whilst the second effects a far more even distribution of wealth throughout the community. The fact that Productive capitalism experiences the same end results at opposite sides of the globe, is a further demonstration that these economic factors are driven by the mechanisms of the financial-industrial system itself rather than merely by cultural factors.

Furthermore, the fact that the social democratic consensus, which brought such prosperity and equity to the post-War world has been breaking down over the past ten years is not a symptom of its intrinsic failure, but rather of its exposure to the attack of aggressive American corporate capitalism, which is striving to take over the world in the spurious name of its particular concept of "freedom." This is yet another reason demonstrating the urgency to throw down the gauntlet in challenging the world cancer of American economic power.

America has always been dismissive of Continental-style capitalism with its link to the social democratic consensus, a system which transcended the in-fighting of mere party politics.

Furthermore, American industrialists and academics on their pay-roll have attempted to deny that the Continental and Far East systems are in any proper sense deserving the designation of "capitalism."

7 – Fall of the Berlin Wall saw the onslaught of America's economic aggression

The two capitalist systems developed, of course, through the force of differing historical circumstances. Productive capitalism only developed in Continental Europe and the Far East as patriarchal fully formed industrial systems during the last quarter of the 19th century; but it was not until the post-War period that it became clearly linked to social democratic values, and even later when there arose any consciousness of a potential conflict between two separate capitalisms.

As long as the Soviet bloc remained in place the Americans dared not challenge nor even whisper a criticism of the financial-industrial systems of their Continental allies; but almost as soon as the Berlin Wall collapsed, using Britain as a springboard, American corporate power was launched aggressively in capturing the control of business in the advanced industrial nations.

With the collapse of the Berlin Wall, America lost no time in asserting her role as the sole surviving world-dominating power, and in conjunction with the intelligentsia, the political-industrial complex assumed an astonishing arrogance with regard to prospects for the future. It was claimed, for example, following the initiative of Francis Fukuyama and his notorious book that The End of History had arrived, by what he meant that the evolution of political theory had reached its apex and no more peaks were to be surmounted. He flattered the American political establishment in the same way that Bossuet, Bishop of Meaux, had flattered the vanity of Louis XIV with his *Histoire Universelle* and other works, after the all-powerful king had striven to crush the liberties of Europe.

Whilst Bossuet asserted a particular brand of Catholicism as a criterion in justifying political power, Francis Fukuyama upheld the ideology of Neo-liberalism and corporate interests as the only path ahead for humanity. With this encouragement, American political power became all the more blatant, and the financial-industrial corporations accelerated their efforts to capture the markets of the world. Added to this is the age-old factor that all power corrupts and that absolute power corrupts absolutely, and since America awoke to find herself free of all competitors, she ruled as absolute in the world of money.

8 – Failure of the counter-attack

Leading Continental economists, such as Michel Albert, let out a cry of pain in warning of what was to follow, but their gestures were powerless; and within several years the press propaganda of the great financial moguls was declaring that the social democratic consensus was doomed to eventual extinction, and that an "intangible" or "unstoppable" global capitalism was to swallow up the industries which had once been particular to nation states.

Because these things were undertaken under the cover of transnational institutions, and because those from many nationalities were drawn into the vortex of something they could not control, there was no mention of the fact that the whirlwind had been summoned originally by the wizards of American corporate power.

The power of globalisation seemed so omnipotent and irreversible that it was accepted as a fact of life which must go unquestioned. But the wizards had blinded the world with a great lie. Under the cover of invisibility, through guile and aggressive tactics, they wormed their way into the power bases of all nation states, in undermining good systems for wealth creation and distribution by replacing them with bad.

9 – A strategy for the future

What, then, is the answer to these problems which seem so insuperable at a first glance? The first step is to raise a consciousness of their existence, and the second is to generate an anger at the theft which has been committed against the tradition of the body politic which had set in place financial and welfare institutions for the benefit of us all. The theft had not so much been that of a robber with a cudgel as that of a pickpocket with a crafty smile and wily fingers, and because of that, we feel all the more vexed at our lack of caution and failure to properly observe the change to our surroundings.

Thirdly, we must examine carefully the exact nature of what has been lost, and then set about its recovery – although not necessarily an exact return to a former situation. Fourthly, we must publicise the cause in building up its support; and fifthly, we must link-in with all friendly political groups and peoples across the world in the unified struggle for justice and equity and the recovery of the economic and cultural integrity of all nation states.

10 – Restoring the lost tradition of social progress

In reference to the third point above, viz., setting about the recovery of what has been lost, this is not a call for a return to a past age, for history moves ahead and what is gone can no more be recovered than can an individual re-live his youth. It is rather a plea for the return of an evolutionary tradition which brought us many benefits, but was cut short through the financial-industrial invasion of a foreign force.

The social democratic consensus which transcended parties of both left and right throughout Europe and amongst the advanced economies of the Far East can never be restored exactly as it existed before, but in challenging the malign power of America, there can and *must* arise another consensus uniting peoples across the political spectrum in creating a world safe for freedom, justice and equity. The basis for such a philosophy, if it is to be meaningful in any scientific sense, must strike at the heart of the socio-economic system and not merely entail a list of good intentions which circulate around the periphery of democratic reality.

At present in the industrialised world parliamentary groups of both left and right do little more than mouth good intentions about poverty, unemployment, climate change, etc., without challenging the need for the radical transformation of those primary institutions which ultimately control the future of us all.

It is the failure to recognise the uselessness of these institutions which reflects back on political parties worldwide so that they too become instruments of failure. For example, the WTO (World Trade Organisation), the World Bank and the IMF (International Monetary Fund) and other institutions associated with the Bretton Woods Agreement were supposedly set-up as international bodies shortly before the end of the last War with the starry-eyed intention of creating a better world for all humanity.

11 – Futility of debt cancellation

It may be asked, then why have they not succeeded? These bodies may be staffed internationally, but in no other sense are they in reality international. For decades they have remained under the financial power of America, and under the false pretence of capitalising the world to raise the standards of the poor, they have done little more than enrich American investors and strengthen American corporations.

These bodies are in no sense charitable organisations but rather instruments of ruthless usury, and are directly responsible for exacerbating poverty, disease, famine and misery throughout the four corners of the globe.

Much talk and even gestures are now made with regard to cancelling world debt, but the debts keep mounting anew after their cancellation. Such gestures make good political capital but they achieve little more than salving the consciences of peoples in the advanced industrial economies. Until the internal operations of the institutions themselves are challenged nothing of lasting benefit can be hoped for the peoples of the Third World. And that is why nothing less than the formulation of a new set of socio-economic doctrines is necessary in challenging the power of America.

12 - Why *privatisation* is a misnomer

What could form the ideological basis for such a set of doctrines, i.e. what idea could hope to fire the imagination and attract peoples in both advanced and developing economies alike? For a diversity of reasons the political ideologies of the past are dead and gone: bankrupted through a combination of their own unworkability and intrinsic faults which oppressed the freedom of the individual.

They make no appeal to thoughtful and intelligent people in the contemporary world, and that is the explanation for the collapse of party political memberships across the spectrum of society in all the advanced economies.

It has been demonstrated that so-called *privatisation* policies are fraudulent because of their outcome, and that the term is in itself a misnomer. It has also been asserted that what is commonly assumed to be the *only* alternative, viz., *nationalisation* or public ownership and control, is unworkable, undesirable, and disastrous to the interests of the majority.

The American establishment with the support of the intelligentsia, as we have shown above, can conceive of no alternative to the above two systems. The American mind is crude and blunt, incapable of observing subtleties or perceiving shades of grey. It represents a critically mindless existence where violent emotions interpret everything in terms of either black or white, for or against, good or evil, friend or foe.

13 – Need for *personalisation* policies

But the non-American world is more thoughtful and sophisticated in its response to change and reality; less stereotyped in its approach to problems; and infinitely more creative in fundamentals, irrespective of whether these concern science, philosophy, or the arts. The ideological concept presented here – and it complements all the realities of the Productive economy as cited above – is that of the *personalisation* of society, and personalisation policies would entail the personalisation of business.

A genuinely free and democratic world cannot exist unless people *as individuals* both own and control the means of production, distribution and exchange. This calls for a reversal of gigantism as promoted in both Soviet Russia and contemporary American, and instead promotes decentralisation policies within and safeguarded by the framework of the nation state.

Whilst the *collectivisation* of the Soviet Union and the *privatisation* of America both in practice crush the aspirations of the individual under the guise of deceptive ideologies, and through the imposition of powerful elites which cannot be effectively challenged through the democratic process, *personalisation* policies are concerned with establishing mechanisms to implement democracy to its furthest practical limits.

14 – What they mean for the poor

Personalisation policies call, firstly, for the worldwide empowerment of peoples through the establishment of extra-legal commercial networks to capitalise the assets of the poor (as described by Hernando de Soto and others), so that the loans or investments of the World Bank or the IMF, etc. (in their present form) would become an unnecessary irrelevance.

Poverty can only be made a thing of the past through making charitable giving a thing of the past, and that is the ultimate purpose of personalisation through the economic empowerment of *individuals* in the mass.

All charity is demeaning to its recipients since it necessarily acknowledges indebtedness to a privileged donor, and every debtor would prefer to be in the shoes of the patron to whom he is held in thrall. The contributor to charity may expect and ask no return or gratitude for his giving, but he nonetheless receives a return. That return entails both the salving of his conscience and the satisfaction of realising his relative comfort and affluence.

But the effect of charity on the donor (and this is in no way intended as a criticism of charitable institutions or their purpose) may be even worse in its moral outcome in that it engenders a thoughtlessness and passive attitude to poverty as an inevitable component of the human condition. Hence the occasional contribution serves to pay off the moral obligation to think through socio-economic issues and search for their resolution.

The old adage, "the poor will always be with us," has become an obscenity in the contemporary world, not only because the assumption is untrue but because the ills of poverty, famine and disease, have been exacerbated through the abuses of corporate power as developed and disseminated by America in conjunction with her industrial allies.

Structural projects for the alleviation and riddance of poverty have now become a practicality in certain parts of the world, usually in central or south America, albeit on a small and patchy scale. But the existence of these isolated projects are being ignored or cold-shouldered by America and the great corporations as they allow no opportunity for profits for themselves.

15 – How America repudiates equal trading rights with the Third world

And furthermore, it may be anticipated that the American establishment will dismiss the concept of personalisation and the economic empowerment of the poor, since they will be seen as endangering the success of her own investment policies.

And such an attack will provide lasting proof that the World Bank, the IMF and the WTO are in no way "charitable institutions" but merely instruments for exploitation and the further enrichment of those who are already rich. Hence these bodies will be unmasked for what they are!

The last thing the American establishment wishes to see is the empowerment of the world's poor, for knowledge, its essential correlative, presages the promise of competition; and as America perceives the world in terms of politically competing as contrasted with cooperating peoples, she is haunted by the fear of this.

She may approve of competition between "equals" but her protectionist policies clearly demonstrate that this is not to be extended to lower level economies. The latter are only to be granted the "privilege" of receiving investments or loans in the distant promise of their future trading equality, and we have already explained the implications of this. America is always intent on retaining her top-dog status and uses all the ruthlessness at her disposal to ensure this.

This is an example of the morally corrupting influence of absolute power – for this is what it is. But there is also an irony in American political thinking and policy, for whilst it is always undertaken in the name of "freedom" and "democracy" it always achieves the opposite.

Such an unconscious hypocrisy could never have arisen unless there was something very wrong with core American values to cause this confusion. This confusion will be explained in greater depth in the third chapter of this book, but meanwhile, we may briefly state that these wrong values accepted by the majority stem from inflated aspirations with regard to the accumulation of wealth linked to the ideal of infinite economic growth, and the belief that the individual is somehow independent of and separate from the community and the state. The vague and impractical aspirations of the pioneering spirit are therefore out of kilter with modern America, or indeed, with the wider world.

16 – Why personal property is necessary for the free individual

The imperative of personalisation policies is to be found in the fact, as argued by Hegel, that the individual can only express his full freedom through the ownership and use of property. The justification for property by the individual is not so much to be found in the fulfilment of needs as for the free expression of the will. This is borne out by the fact that more enjoyment is derived through choice in the *use* of property than through the purely utilitarian function in its fulfilment of *need*, and it is only through the use of property that the personality is expressed.

The individual as an isolated being is nothing, and it is only in relation to material surroundings, and more significantly, the control and ownership of possessions that personality is developed.[4] For these reasons, property should be held as a human right in the same way as other basic rights already established through legislation in free societies.

The right to personal property, in both the domestic and business spheres of life, is vital for the free individual since it represents ultimate power and status in the community, not as a negative factor (as politicised by Old Socialists) but as a positive and constructive factor impacting on the general good of society.

Personalisation policies require the existence of smaller scale business whenever these may be made viable, for the outcome is not only greater competition and choice for consumers, but more significantly, the *greater* empowerment of more people, and a general raising of intelligence levels and socio-political consciousness throughout the community. It is also a step towards a greater egalitarianism, but not an egalitarianism of a dependent and fatalistic class at the base of the community but rather of decision-makers comprising the middle-middle majority.

Personalisation is helped by decentralisation or regionalisation policies, so that industrial investment credit

---

[4] See especially, Hegel's *Philosophy of Right*, trans. by T.M. Knox, OUP, 1952, pp. 235-236.

banks and local authorities may promote appropriate bodies for funding business and training personnel.

It is no coincidence that the most democratic economies worldwide have almost invariably sprung from smaller population countries; whilst the most oppressive or socially polarised regimes are usually found amongst the largest and most populous peoples. This is because gigantism is so often anathema to the spirit of democracy, and it seems that scale alone may in certain circumstances transmute sound and healthy societies into inequitable economies of injustice and division.

17 – Need to stage development in the Third World

In Third World countries personalisation policies are dictated partly by the need for *staging* development so preventing the catastrophic social consequences of sudden massive inward investment which so often destroys overnight successful (albeit backward) self-subsistent communities. When that occurs great numbers are driven from their rural landholdings of one type or another, and vast new proletariats are created in shanty towns.

To prevent such unfortunate consequences, intermediate technologies need to be developed, but such projects are rarely of interest to the great American corporations, or the World Bank, or the IMF or the WTO, since the returns are so minimal to investors.

This is particularly applicable in the sphere of agriculture. The great corporations are intent on promoting cash crops in developing the poorer countries, but nothing could be more disastrous in further impoverishing the poor, or in damaging the environment through the wasteful exhaustion of fossil fuels through the consequent international trading of such goods. Cash crops are intended for export to the First World with earnings for the Third World, but in practice such earnings remain predominantly in the pockets of wealthy landowners or the investing corporations.

Colin Tudge has authoritatively written that, "there is the huge and all-pervasive mistake, which says that Africa and the developing world in general, could solve their problems if only world trade were truly free.   What nonsense. ... If Africa industrialised its farms, that would throw most of its people out of work, and it cannot industrialise without foreign investment, which entails foreign control. ... The task is not to twiddle with World Trade Organisation rules or even to ease up on debt, but to rethink. In the short term, the prime task for the world as a whole, and Africa in particular, must be to build on traditional agriculture, which alone can maintain landscapes and provide good jobs for the billions who need them: with appropriate-tech, small-scale financial support, and the general ambition not to trash small farms, but to make agrarian life tolerable, and indeed positively agreeable and desirable."[5]

Then, again, intermediate technologies or Gandhi-like or village industries employing existing labour and skills on a more organised basis, are best promoted through the internal capitalisation of the assets of the poor in conjunction with extra-legal commercial networks for ensuring personal ownership rights and the enforcement of contracts.

Business malpractices and widespread dishonesty of every conceivable kind are found in most developing and very poor communities, and so order needs to be created out of anarchy. To achieve this, educational projects must be embarked upon to change attitudes with regard to trade and the negotiating of agreements, and as soon as the rewards of prosperity are experienced, old ways will give way to new.

18 – Personalisation policies in industrially advanced economies

In industrially advanced countries, too, personalisation policies will be welcomed for the benefits they bring. In the private sphere, in regard to the blessings of ownership, we have

---

[5] Colin Tudge, What Matters More Than Anything Else is Agriculture, *New Statesman*, 11th July 2005, p. 21. See also his book, *So Shall We Reap*, Penguin, 2005.

already referred to these; but in the consumer sphere, the benefits will be reflected in greater diversity in the high street, greater choice, and a business community more committed to and more closely connected with immediate localities.

A more human scale will help towards a greater bonding and sense of belonging between the different functional groups of business, local government, the professions, and servicing institutions as schools, colleges, hospitals and the police. It will also help to diminish the occurrence of corruption and backhanders in a society when powerful corporations jostle with one another in trying to buy their way into a locality by twisting the arms of Planning officers and elected representatives for lucrative contracts.

There are, of course, industrial sectors which are necessarily large in scale, such as car manufacturing, heavy chemicals, shipbuilding or mining, but these too lend themselves to personalisation through the amendment of company law, and implementing co-determination and share-ownership policies. A legal stake in the part-management and ownership of enterprises by shop-floor workers is also an assurance towards greater industrial efficiency, and so an added benefit for senior management and investors.

Indeed, Japan has proven a world leader in successful industrial relations through her Quality Circles and organisational decision-making from the bottom up. Employees who feel valued and are called-upon for their advice and ideas on better efficiency are more committed and reliable than their slave-like counterparts in American industry who are inveigled by the Behaviourist practices of Taylorism to act like zombies at their masters' behest. America is a country of illusive freedom where *real* rights are denied, and the clever practices of Behaviourism are reflected in John Updike's contention that, "America is a vast conspiracy to make you happy."[6]

Whilst the Japanese worker has traditionally in the post-War period been a life-long employee of an organisation where all are striving towards a common purpose, and freely accepts

---

[6] John Updike, *Problems*, How To Love America & Leave It At The Same Time, 1980.

this as the will of all; the American worker is no more than a temporary cog in the wheel, subject to the will of an organisation with which he has little common purpose.

Consequently, the American worker is not only alienated, but resentful and uncertain of the future. He is in no sense *his own master* beyond the simple right of relinquishing his employment. Personalisation policies are therefore not merely intended to create a feel-good factor, but through legal mechanisms, to ensure the undying commitment of employees to a common purpose transcending the transience of the personal profit nexus.

19 – Why international power today is economic but not democratic

How are personalisation policies and other measures for freedom, justice and equity, to be achieved internationally in a very diverse world? They cannot be achieved unless recognition is first given to the need for the cultural and economic integrity of peoples and their nation states. This is because the nation in practice still remains the ultimate democratic authority in expressing the will of peoples, and as yet there exist no effective mechanisms for international bodies to transcend that will.

This is partly why international institutions have proven so weak or unsatisfactory as political bodies; although the greater reason for their limitations is their corruption or absorption by the vested interests of transnational corporations.

Hence the sad fact remains that whilst democratic power is still circumscribed by the boundaries of the nation state, the vested interests of unaccountable rentier or global capitalism have succeeded triumphantly in the international sphere without encountering any opposition of note. Whilst the World Bank and the IMF are prime examples of such a takeover, the United Nations may be cited as an example of where power, both economic and political, has simply been withdrawn with the inevitable consequences of weakening its function.

These are the reasons why people power still has to be mediated through the democratic organisations of nation states if it hopes to be truly effective and long-term internationally. Each country – even those of almost identical backgrounds – differ widely with regard to their perception of how similar problems should be resolved. This is because political groups and traditions, and modes of thinking, differ slightly in each country, and consequently, the implementation of practical measures are undertaken in very different ways.

The preparedness of peoples to commit themselves to a cause is therefore expressed according to existing living standards, varying levels in the spirit of collective generosity, and differing emphases on the perception of those causes, etc. A people or nation cannot and should not be pushed by international forces beyond their natural toleration level. Quiet persuasion is the most that can be hoped for in achieving best results.

Amity and constructive cooperation between nations is best achieved through respecting the cultural and economic integrity of peoples, and it should be borne in mind that this appeal for world resistance to American power has been evoked by a country with almost no respect for the democratic will of those beyond her own frontiers.

20 – Defining Economic Integrity

The principle of economic integrity begins with the natural need of a country to maintain its self-subsistence interests, followed by the need to protect those primary industries or benefits derived from geography.

It is an absurdity, for example, for a country to import foodstuffs and other basic products she can better produce herself. Outrageous distortions in exchange rates between countries which seem to justify the "profitability" of mutually criss-crossing the same goods across the globe, brings benefit to none except traders, and does much to damage the environment through the exhaustion of fossil fuels through unnecessary transportation.

Good farmland should be put to productive use for the benefit of local communities, and not condemned as set-aside in satisfying the corporate interests of transnational organisations. Mountains and hillsides should be utilised for afforestation purposes purposes or viable hill-farming, and not wasted as mere hunting playgrounds, or allowed to remain idle as the vast unproductive estates of absent super-rich landlords.   If the market for organic produce demands that more land should be cultivated, and that a greater labour intensity in the industry should follow it its wake, then economic mechanisms should be put in place to ensure commercial viability in fulfilling such needs.

It is nonsense to argue contrariwise, i.e. that the marketing or democratic demands of a people cannot be fulfilled on the grounds of their non-viability. The reality should be understood that the arguments of the *economics establishment* are no less "ideological" than the doctrines of religion. There is laziness amongst those in power to comprehend the possibilities for change, and the decision-making of the powerful in conjunction with accepted custom soon tends to become entrenched as the permanent situation of things.

Economic integrity also includes the need of every country to protect the interests of its secondary (i.e. manufacturing) and tertiary (i.e. service) industries. The demands of international competition and free markets are justified when these mean access to better quality and even less costly products, but when the point is reached that entire swathes of industry are swiped into oblivion, then the time has come for reassessment. It was once argued in Britain that the demise of manufacturing was of little consequence since we could always rely on the service industries. But when these too fly overseas and there is nothing left of wealth creating significance, a country is in *real* trouble with regard to its future.

The first symptom of economic catastrophe is experienced when capital flight is attracted into the passive assets of land and property, and unrealistic and unaffordable values are reached depriving huge population sectors from the benefits of ownership. This is quickly followed by the polarisation of society between rich and poor and all the social ills which follow from that. For these reasons it is the duty of the state to protect manufacturing as a sound base for the service industries, so that the two sectors in conjunction with the primary occupations of forestry, farming, fishing, etc., may cooperate effectively for national wealth creation. This calls for a policy of selective import controls or strategic protectionism in ensuring the existence of balanced economies serving the needs of the majority.

21 – But this opposed by American power

The strength of the rentier economy is to be found in the overweening confidence of the vested interests of the great corporations, and their insistence that only *their* ways are workable or justified in pursuing the common good. The nonsense of such convictions are in part demonstrated by the fact that some of the most richly endowed countries in natural resources are at the same time amongst the poorest in the world (note Nigeria and other African countries), whilst some of the worst endowed countries in natural resources are also the wealthiest (note the Netherlands or Japan).

Hence, if countries concentrated more on maintaining their economic integrity the inevitable outcome would be a fairer distribution of the world's wealth. And in that is to be found the imperative of liberating the world from American economic domination.

The liberation of the world from America is best achieved through an organisation which works on two levels: firstly, through creating a voluntary association with national organisations under a controlling international head office; and secondly, through establishing governmental agencies through parliamentary channels, which would eventually initiate an official international headquarters, or utilise an existing body such as a department of the United Nations.

Both voluntary and governmental organisations within each nation state would be self-determining in their policies. This is necessary because of the huge diversity of political systems and beliefs throughout the globe, and it also explains why the international HQ of such an association needs to have a scatter-gun approach in its appeal to the peoples of the world.

22 – Internal capitalisation versus rentier exploitation

The overall purpose of a movement in freeing the world from America, however, would remain the struggle against economic imperialism, defined in terms of transnational investments or loans threatening to either the economic or cultural integrity of states.

In place of this would be mutual trade, or the bartering of products and services mediated through a Productive capitalist system; and assistance for developing economies would be promoted through the export of skills for *internal* capitalisation. This would take the form of bankers, lawyers, business people, teachers, doctors, etc., from the first world settling and working in the Third World to raise the living standards of the poor and oppressed.

This would be financed through a mixture of first world charity and Third World taxation, to ensure the staged development from intermediate to advanced technological status, without the intervening upheaval which so often disrupts the stability and livelihoods of peoples in traditional societies. Extra-legal systems would be put in place in empowering the wealth-creating assets of the poor, and consultants and business advisers would be on hand to ensure a smooth transition from the old ways to the new.

Meanwhile, higher bodies of learning would be founded for teaching political theory, social ethics, business management, etc., so that rational attitudes would be imparted to all functional groups in creating societies based on justice, equity, and democratic ideals.

23 – Flunkeyism never gains respect

In conclusion it has to be emphasised that America holds all peoples and nations in thrall – and not only the poor and oppressed – and her closest allies are held in most contempt of all. No country has been treated with more disdain by the world bully in the post-War period than Great Britain. Whilst British governments have offered America favour after favour, they have gained almost nothing in return – apart from empty promises for lucrative contracts which never materialised.

Whilst Britain has sacrificed the lives of her young men in useless foreign adventures at the behest of the US, the latter has embargoed the importation of British goods over petty trading squabbles. When Britain has needed to borrow in times of crisis, or when fighting for her survival, America has only lent with a grudging heart and on usurious terms which touched the limits of bankrupting the recipient – and then she has expected gratitude for her exploitation. Meanwhile, in a trading situation, she has almost invariably adopted a non-negotiable position.

If this is friendship then what is enmity? The astonishing fact is that for decades British ministers and civil servants seemed hardly to comprehend the extent of their own flunkeyism. This was either because they were dazzled by the dollars of a superpower, or were simply pushed into a corner through their own weakness.

There is, however, another factor which part explains the one-sided and degrading friendship between the monolith and its hanger-on. Britain, like the US, is also a rentier economy – usually referred to as partners in the Anglo-Saxon mode of capitalism. Britain has therefore long been a testing ground or springboard for American-type capitalism before establishing its many projects, services, or diversified ventures throughout the rest of the world. In this perhaps is to be found the real cornerstone of the so-called "special relationship," but it has brought little benefit to the majority of British people.

There is, of course, a difference of degree between the rentier capitalism of Britain and that of the US, for the latter is more aggressive and deceitful in its style and content, although in Britain over the past 40 years, both the financial-industrial infrastructure and the marketing of financial services have been transformed out of all recognition.   Gone is the gentlemanly capitalism of a past era with its stability, the steady hand of experience, and trust in the integrity of those of good character; and in have come the yuppies and wide-boys with their unprincipled risk-taking, their rat-race style of buying and selling, and their oblivious and irresponsible attitude to the end-purpose of the industry.

24 – Why Britain should lead the initiative for world freedom

Britain's past involvement with the US in the pursuit of socially damaging Rentier capitalism is a good reason for her leading the initiative in the world's struggle for freedom from America.   This is because of her practical experience and knowledge of what the Rentier economy means in undermining the entire industrial infrastructure of a nation.

Is not the collapse of British manufacturing in the post-War period accountable solely to the fallibility of the system when put in competition with the Productive economies of Continental Europe and the Far East?   We have certainly demonstrated this contention in some depth in several of our books.

Likewise, has not America also experienced the decimation of her manufacturing base through competition with Japan?   America's industrial strength now only lies with her armaments industry, and so unwittingly she has put herself on a war footing which she is obliged to fulfil through seeking out the illusion of ever-more "windmills" for destruction.[7]

The rhetoric of "peace" and "democracy" and the "war against terrorism" are merely cries of desperation in the need to keep the tanks and bombers rolling off the production lines. America is entrapped within a tangle of political and military commitments arising from the mutation of her economy into an irreversible war machine, and only the collapse of her economy from within is likely to reverse these malign trends.

Britain is therefore burdened with the unwelcome responsibility of acting as a kind of bridge between the Rentier economy of the US and that of the Productive economies of the industrialised world.   As an EU member, and no less significantly, because of her post-War political tradition of welfare as a benevolent state, she is obliged on balance to commit her fate with her European partners for the better future of humanity. For all these reasons, and most of all in defending her integrity as a self-respecting state, she cannot evade the categorical imperative of throwing down the gauntlet at the feet of the American tyrant in defending the freedom of the world.

*

---

[7] In this context it is apt to quote John Le Carré when he wrote, "How Bush and his junta succeeded in deflecting America's anger from Bin Laden to Saddam Hussein is one of the great conjuring tricks in history," *Time*, 27th January 2003.

CHAPTER 2

AMERICA AND THE DECEPTION OF THE WORLD

*"I am willing to Love all mankind, except an American. ...
Rascals – Robbers - Pirates."*

Dr. Samuel Johnson, Wednesday 15th April 1778.

1 – Why anti-Americanism is necessary

Except temporarily, during periods of actual war, an all-out campaign against any people or nation cannot ordinarily be justified, and neither is it likely to attract the cooler mind of the good-natured majority. But the present power relationships of the world with America not only justifies such a campaign but makes it an imperative – irrespective of our subjective personal feelings and how they may change from day-to-day or even from hour-to-hour. This is not only because of the huge and ubiquitous and ever-increasing domination of America in the fields of politics, finance, trade, and culture, but because that domination conflicts with the wishes, the interests, and integrity of so many peoples, and furthermore, is a domination which is often misguided and intrinsically wrong from every viewpoint.

An underlying anti-Americanism, expressed in a variety of forms, found amongst peoples throughout the globe reflects resentments and tensions based on genuine grounds for discontent. Anti-Americanism can no longer be dismissed as merely the natural or human envy of those seemingly stronger or more successfully placed than themselves; nor because of an over-bearing attitude like that of an older or bigger relative; nor even simply because Americans may be so different from ourselves in attracting ridicule or disdain. Substantive issues lie at the root of anti-American feeling, which reflects honest bias rather than unfair prejudice, and these touch on things which affect our pockets, restrict our choice, contradict our political ideals, make nonsense of our economic values on waste or the environment, or otherwise shock our valid susceptibilities.

The outbreak of the war against Iraq, together with the clear indication of further wars to follow, has finally tipped the balance. The fact that benefits may result from such wars is irrelevant. We are talking here of a dangerous precedent in allowing a superpower to launch unauthorised acts of aggression. In examining the recent history of that superpower, there is nothing to suggest that such aggression is not motivated by anything other than determination to pursue its own commercial advantage at the expense of vulnerable nations. That alone (and there are many other causes of complaint) justifies the need for launching a democratic movement against America and everything she stands for.

Everything she stands for? That phrase may raise some eyebrows! Yes, everything she stands for in the sense of unwanted domination and influence over smaller or weaker peoples unable to confront the sheer might of her power, and everything in the sense of promoting a valid generalisation as opposed to the individuality or specificity of American life. Anything less than an uncompromising challenge to everything she means would merely open up chinks in our defensive armour to the dialectical ingenuity and persistence of her advocates. And in any case, what does America really represent? The so-called "American dream" of the pioneering promise of infinitely available wealth is just seen as a farcical mirage by anyone outside her borders. The spirit giving rise to such optimism is no more than castles floating on clouds.

2 – The fraud of American democracy

And as for American democracy, that stands as a still greater delusion! A close examination of the American political system, and how parties are controlled, and how representatives of the people are actually put in place would reveal that America is in reality a plutocracy. The electoral systems of America –

and they are applied to many more government offices than found elsewhere – amount to no more than sleight of hand in placing appointees of powerful financial interests. And if a democratic society or democratic ideals are supposed to emerge from the benefits of democratic government, then the results are worse still. A society which is polarised between rich and poor as no other in the world's wealthiest countries; a society with no safety net for those losing their employment, or their good health, or encountering accident or injury; a society which does not support the poor or those beyond the age of retirement; and a society with the highest percentage of criminals and prisoners in the world, defies the very ethos of democracy.

It is astonishing when noted public figures so often refer to America as the "world's leading democracy," or the "only remaining champion for freedom," for such talk is made in ignorance. Have these people actually defined freedom or analysed the American political system before opening their mouths? No! They have simply been overcome by the idea of America's size together with the meaningless label which shouts the word "Democracy!" By all means let us identify those nations which promote the reality of freedom and democracy and then sing their praises, but the criterion of size will be of little help in the search. Almost nothing of value is to be learned from America with regard to the ideals or practice of democracy.

The greatest democracies which may stand as an example for us all are to be found in north west Europe, e.g. Sweden, the Netherlands, Finland, Switzerland, Belgium, Germany, France, etc. It is the administrative and financial-industrial systems (in their pure uncorrupted forms) of these countries which need to be studied in depth in ensuring justice and equity for the peoples of the world. If special note is to be made of those countries which have vastly raised the educational standards and material expectations of their peoples, within an egalitarian framework whilst democracy has tended to lag behind, then the Far East Tigers must be upheld as a desirable paradigm – not forgetting the coastal provinces of post-1978 China. Many more instructive lessons may be learned by developing countries from Singapore, or Taiwan, or Korea, than from the USA which is prone to teach the bad habits of corruption and money-greed than the values of study and hard work. If statistical data is to be used in measuring the lawfulness of a people, then those of the Far East Tigers may be put on a pedestal of virtue by comparison with the degraded inhabitants of the superpower. So much then for American democracy!

3 – The charlatanry of her foreign policy

Meanwhile, the foreign policy of America, and this directly affects all the peoples of the world, is a mixture of naivety, incompetence, charlatanry, inexplicable contradictions, and spiteful revanchism, astounding to behold. Budding democracies have been crushed, one-time allies mysteriously betrayed, fearsome dictators placed in power, and millions sent to their deaths through the expediency of shareholders' profits, and all these things have been promoted nominally in the cause of democracy, but in reality to enhance the dollar and America's trading advantage. The psychological perceptions of her rulers in terms of the need to pit Virtue against Evil, and the clumsy consequences of this, reflects a primitive view of human nature which is pre-Enlightenment in its crudity. The bigotry of her Bible-bashing fundamentalist ruling elite not only defies commonsense, but modernity, ethics, humanity, and a sociological understanding of society.

None of the above could have occurred without the extraordinary self-confidence and arrogance of America and her people towards the rest of the world. It is an arrogance which equals that of the post-Alexandrine Greek or the post-Augustan Roman, in societies which ruled the entire known world, as America now dominates the present. It reflects not only an assumed but unspoken sense of superiority, but a conviction that their political system is not only transcendent but incapable of further perfection. This view is developed in *The End of History* by the Japanese-American, Francis Fukuyama, a book which elaborates the stunningly presumptuous thesis that with the fall of the Berlin Wall, Neo-American Liberalism was the sole remaining political ideology of any significance, whose destiny is to absorb the peoples of the world within its beneficent embrace.

The thesis assumes that the human intellect, or political circumstances, are incapable of further development or diversity, and hence the end of history as a political evolutionary process. This is a perception which may be held in America, in a politically highly homogeneous society, where democracy has long since atrophied and party political supporters are no longer thinking individuals but hired automatons or cheerleaders at boozy conventions. But to assume that such a situation pertains anywhere outside their own country shows a crass ignorance of the world, and an incomprehensible undervaluation of the human imagination and creativity in responding to the challenges of social organisation.

4 – Her gung-ho militarism

The prerogative of American military force is based on the sheer might of her financial-industrial infrastructure, but in a world which aspires to justice and equity – in addition to democracy, it is doubtful if America deserves her status as a mediating military power, or as the so-called global peacemaker. Her gung-ho, trigger-happy troops, with their jumpy response to any spectre in the shadows, are characteristics reflecting badly on the reputation of any army. The space-age technology of her armed services has not come up to scratch, or more probably, is incompetently used, but nothing can excuse the cavalier disregard for the Geneva Convention in the failure to protect the civilian population, *vis-à-vis* access to medical attention; or the euphemistically termed frequency of "friendly fire;" or the close-range shelling of hotel tower blocks and the wanton killing of foreign journalists; or worse still, the senseless slaughter of innocent civilians seeking shelter in the neutral haven of their own homes.

These characteristics of the American armed services are not a recent development, but are long-entrenched in her traditional modes of warfare. As a British soldier serving in the 50s, I encountered many comrades-in-arms returning from the Korean conflict, who had nothing but reproach for the Americans alongside whom they fought, and always the criticism was the same: boastfulness and bravado interspersed with timidity and a too-ready wasteful use of automatic gunfire. For these reasons (amongst others) public opinion should be harnessed for the withdrawal of the American armed services from all foreign territories. Their replacement, under the auspices of the UN, should be with troops more serenely self-assured, such as from Sweden, the Netherlands, or Eire, or from Britain. The outstanding quality of *contemporary* British troops, as the peacemakers of the world, has been forged in such difficult and unenviable assignments as those in Bosnia or Northern Ireland, where their varied skills have proven them as the finest anywhere available in the delicate task of laying the foundations for justice and democracy.

5 – The rule of the philistines

The problem of America's cultural domination gives, perhaps, rise to greater resentment than any other aspect of her power – certainly amongst peoples in the more developed countries in both East and West. George Clemenceau, who lived for several years in America, and therefore spoke from experience, stated that, "America is the only country in history which miraculously has gone directly from barbarism to degeneration without the usual interval of civilisation."[8]

There is something unique in the jarring to the senses of so-called American culture. It is an unpleasantly shared experience amongst all peoples in a very diverse world, and yet it is an experience which is felt in the same way despite this diversity. There is no other country on earth which arouses such

---

[8]   Quoted by John Micklethwait & Adrian Wooldridge in, *A Future Perfect: The Challenge & Hidden Promise of Globalisaton,* Heineman, 2000, p. 188.

universal feelings of disdain, ridicule, revulsion, and resentment at the vulgarity and philistinism of her life style and culture, which seems to intrude and corrupt, like an insidious cancer, on other life styles and peoples in bringing them to the gutter. What is it that has given rise to such a horrible way of life? Why is it that the Americans appear so very objectionable, in the generality, in every aspect of their existence?   There is the crying need for a research paper to analyse and explain these urgent questions.

These are the reasons why an international movement must be launched against America and what she does, and such a movement must call for close and friendly co-operation amongst the peoples of the world if it is to succeed in its purpose.

But there is another level on which a campaign for *Freedom From America* needs to exist. It may be suggested – argued even – that such a campaign would promote a hidden agenda. After all, the campaign against America is not solely because of what she is *per se*, but because of what she represents, and moreover, exports to the rest of the world. It is these specific qualities which are the cause of objection, and as they spread their tentacles throughout the globe, they are no longer exclusive to the source of their origin. Is America, therefore, to be made the scapegoat for qualities or tendencies found throughout the world for which, after all, she is not entirely responsible in the first place? No, for that would be unfair.

6 – How "presidential" government is replacing democratic government

Nonetheless, she may excusably be used as a catalyst in reinvigorating political life where the latter has atrophied or died a death. In the industrialised world whilst ennui has suffused party political life, political feelings remain strong yet strangely unexpressed in organised revolt. Due to powerful yet unseen shifts in the political tectonic plates of socio-economic systems in recent decades, the public have become alienated from their feeling of empowerment in the democratic process. As this has resulted from slow as contrasted with dramatic change there is no resentment at this loss of power, just a passive acceptance of its occurrence. But if you doubt the reality of its outcome just compare the political self-confidence of the voter in the 1950s with the cynicism and helplessness of his counterpart in the year 2006.

And how has this powerlessness come about – for it does not simply reflect a change of feeling or mental attitude – since its causes are rooted in real and underlying changes in the industrial system? There is today a far greater concentration of capital and ownership in fewer hands; a huge process of gentle dispossession, and the creation of a dependent chief executive and managerial class with little control over its future; a hugely enlarged intervention of corporate business into the affairs of government; the sidelining of parliament or elected representatives to a position of impotence; the cancerous growth of undemocratic and unaccountable NGOs with their own agendas; and an increase of power by the premier and his inner cabinet in a huddle with a posse of unelected cronies. The descriptive outcome of the resulting style of government from all these tendencies is *Presidential*.

Presidential, in this sense, refers to the American system, and it is an apt description. The Presidential style of government does not necessarily – at a first glance – convey to the political lay person an impression which is undemocratic or authoritarian, for the reason of the simplistic and stereotypical association that everything connected with the American administration must somehow be democratic. But that is not the case. Presidential government increasingly undermines the foundations of democracy, and this is more true of countries outside America than within the USA itself. What is the explanation for this? America is to blame for the spread of Presidential styles of government throughout the industrialised world, but not in the way that might at first be thought.

7 – But corporate power is more wide-ranging

The *direct* influence of America in changing governmental systems in advanced economies has not been considerable, although the American influence on Tony Blair, Gordon Brown, and others, on how to control electorates and sideline inconvenient opposition should not be dismissed as entirely negligible. The *real* influence of America is exerted through the indomitable power of her transnational corporations, and the ruthless modes of financial services which follow in their wake, and it is these things which transform existing institutions and force changes on the style of government. The reason that the Presidential style of government is often more malign in countries outside America than within is because, as noted above, the USA at least enjoys the benefit of more elected offices and counter-checks than most other countries, even though they are only juggled between powerful financial interests.

The spread of so-called Presidential government is therefore a bane throughout the world, undermining the effective representation of those without power, and poisoning both democratic movements and the established ideals of civil service departments. Everywhere principles are sacrificed for expediency and pragmatism, so that powerful corporate interests may predominate over the will and needs of the majority. Even the funding of the British Labour Party is being sourced from corporations with agendas of their own, whilst traditional contributions from the trade unions are either falling away or contracting from year to year.

In 1991 the eminent French economist, Michel Albert, saw the publication of his book, *Capitalism Against Capitalism*, in Paris. The book enumerated the dire social consequences of Neo-American capitalism, and was written as a warning shot to the countries of Continental Europe against its off-shoot, Thatcherism, vaulting across the Channel and undermining the post-War social democratic consensus which had so successfully taken root. Since then much has transpired. The warning was not sufficient to ward off the juggernaut of American capitalism. Thatcherism, as a reluctantly accepted ideology, together with the entrenchment of American big business, has now won the day. The results are not only a declining productive economy and falling living standards, but cut-backs in health and social services, unemployment benefit, and poorer prospects for pensioners' incomes throughout the Continent and Scandinavia.

8 – American-style finance has undermined Japan

Meanwhile in Japan, the decision to up-date or Americanise their financial institutions, which had been so successful for so long in the financing of industry through credit investment banks of various kinds, was to lead to economic disaster. The changes entailed a new ideological approach, for the traditional mode of deficit financing (also undertaken with phenomenal success throughout Western Continental Europe and amongst the other Far East Tigers) was anathema to the thinking of American capitalism with its insistence on equity or stock exchange funding, and the usurious emphasis of making money out of money. The Americans have always seen deficit financing as somehow bucking the free market, or copping out of the capitalist system, on the grounds that the *real* purpose of the capitalist process is the maximisation of investors' profit alone, to which all other aspects of business should be strictly subordinated.

But the Japanese were seduced by the prospects of unprecedented money profits by these new ideas from across the Pacific, and fell in with the proposals presented. The consequences led to a mad rush of share buying; an inflation of property values as capital fled into passive assets and out of investment in productivity; and finally to a crash which ruined millions of ordinary investors and bankrupted thousands of enterprises. All this so damaged the economy that it looked as if Japan would never recover her former pre-eminence.

9 – Need to politicise the underlying economic issues

None of the above issues have been politicised in any proper sense, i.e. analysed and taken up by parliamentary groups and presented as problems to be directly confronted. It is true that globalisation has been identified by innumerable groups, and that millions have been organised to demonstrate against its malign consequences, but such opposition has been muddled or confused with other peripheral (although admittedly important) issues, such as threats to the environment. Demonstrations against globalisation have been negative in that few constructive alternatives have been presented – or if they have, they have tended towards the utopian. This is because an in-depth understanding of financial-industrial systems and how to change them has been lacking, and consequently, the anti-globalisation movement has ultimately remained impotent, and so no real source of significant apprehension to the giant transnational corporations who just continue in their bad old ways as before.

All these problems are complex in that they concern issues which are neither purely economic, nor political, nor technological, nor the preserve of vested interest groups, but are a mixture of all four, and so they cannot be reduced to pat explanations which immediately satisfy the understanding of the lay person. The latter is liable to see these problems as abstruse or abstract, and more significantly, is impatient of attempting an understanding. In the light of knowledge and the necessity of protracted explanation, however, these problems may be presented with crystal clarity to the layman if he only has the time and patience to listen.[9] But to the modern politician, who has become too accustomed to the essential word-bite and convenient spin, the idea of a lengthy explanation to his electors calls for more energy than he is prepared to give. Communication between the lay person and the politician

---

[9] All these issues are discussed in some depth in my books, *The Spirit of New Socialism and the end of Class-based Politics*; *Reinventing Democratic Socialism for People Prosperity*; *New Socialist Business Values for Industrial Resurgence*; and, *Foundations of New Socialism a vision for the third millennium*, all published by Arena Books.

becomes problematical when both tend towards a mental laziness in examining the vital aspects of an issue, and too often this leads to a distortion of the truth or to outright lying.

It can, however, be well asserted that the problems of globalisation originate from and are maintained by the American capitalist system. When the world fails to comprehend the nature of globalisation, and how it undermines the material welfare of peoples in both the industrialised economies and developing territories, America may be said, through a sleight of hand, to have inflicted a deceit on the world. There is a kind of magic when the temptress, the wicked witch, comes forward with the promise of happiness and prosperity, only to strip away what fortune remained in the first place – and the victims are left stupid and confused as to how it came about.

10 – How America won her reputation as a benevolent superpower

In explaining this misplaced trust, something must be said about the historical circumstances which created the picture of America as the benevolent donor and fount of democracy. In the immediate post-War period America did facilitate the re-building of Continental Europe through the assistance of the Marshall Plan, and the civil and military American authorities did play a significant role in returning democracy to a war-torn West Germany, despite widespread policy disagreements amongst all four occupying powers. Meanwhile in Japan, the American occupation forces under General Douglas MacArthur, played successfully a vital part in democratising the country despite difficulties and criticism in encountering such a formidable task.

But all that was in the immediate post-War period, and achieved in the aftermath and tensions of a destructive war and the idealistic hopes for a sunny future. Most of all, such beneficent gestures were motivated by the fear of Communism, or the Soviet axis. But with time, all was to change, and America's financial-industrial establishment not only changed in meeting the demands for increasing returns on investment, but began to harden its approach in its commercial relationships with the outside world. Within a decade the philanthropic mask had fallen entirely, a new generation of hard-faced men in the fields of finance, politics, and intelligence, had formed an alliance to further the interests of the American investor, and to claim their pound of flesh in compensating for the weak-mindedness of the past. It was in this commercial culture that the malign aspects of globalisation first began to develop as we know them today.

11 – And how she lost it

Globalisation is seen by many as something omnipresent and nebulous, as inevitable and permanent. It is seen as unchallengeable for the simple reason of its ubiquity and lack of any point at which an attack may be directed, almost as if the invisibility of the wind was to be confronted absurdly by the sharpened swords of an army. If, however, globalisation is identified for what it really is as a phenomenon specific to America, the problem is clarified and made concrete in a way which meets the understanding of the dullest intellect. The largest corporations may be described, their histories told, and how step-by-step, they penetrated the different territories of the world, and how groups of individuals manipulated markets, set in motion usurious systems, accumulated profits for themselves, tricked the owners of land and productive enterprises, and ruthlessly exploited entire economies.

The topic must be made sufficiently concrete to touch the senses in a way that generalisations or the abstract elucidation of economic principles never can. If America had never existed it is inconceivable that globalisation could ever have come into being, for so many factors specific to that country needed to coalesce in making it a reality: e.g., particular types of investing activity; enterprises of a sufficient size and number; political institutions encouraging extra-fast growth irrespective of its repercussions on existing patterns of social organisation; an expansive pioneering culture uninhibited by regulation; and an aversion to any kind of collectivism which restrains capital accumulation for any reason whatsoever.

Only in America have such socio-economic conditions arisen and coalesced to make globalisation not merely possible but inevitable. For example, in China which currently looks to being the world's chief beneficiary of globalisation in the longer term, globalisation could never have originated because of *guanxi* or personal connections, and the family-oriented culture of Chinese business which restricts its size, whereby even the largest enterprises do not threaten the economic foundations of society. Once these facts are understood and comparisons made between the very different socio-economic systems of other peoples, values may be identified which separate out the pros and cons of various supporting economic mechanisms. Choices then become apparent and different ways emerge for the successful organisation of free markets.

12 – The futility of inter-party strife within nations

There is a further aspect of the need for anti-Americanism which must be touched upon. If countries look to their underlying socio-economic problems, their solution cannot be found from within their borders or within the remit of their government's discretion, even though every honest means may be made in the attempt. Undesirable as the reality may be, inter-party strife within nations as a means to the resolution of issues is today little more than jousting at windmills. However misguided the aims or purposes of the Tory Party – or any other party – the matter is relevant no more. If the Tory Party is in tatters, or the "quiet man" is unheard,[10] this is no more than a reflection of the intuitive realisation amongst the electorate that all party politics has been sidelined by those more powerful forces described above.

And those forces have corrupted party politics with a self-imposed – an obligatory illusion (to serve their very survival), as

---

[10] Reference to Iain Duncan-Smith.

to the importance and motivating power of democratic systems which they no longer have.   But the illusion has to be kept up, as otherwise the dreadful truth would be out that the people have no influence whatsoever over their political future.   Hence in purifying and reinvigorating democratic life anti-Americanism has become an essential tool in identifying *real* or underlying issues and linking them as crucial questions for party political debate.

13 – Anti-Americanism is necessary in concretising complex socio-economic issues

The first step in concretising these complex financial-industrial problems is the need for promoting anti-Americanism, not merely in identifying their source and substantiality, but of more significance, in arousing sufficient interest in the first place amongst the general public.   The public love to have their feelings aroused, and not least by hatred, or the presentation of a hate figure.   If the ills of globalisation are therefore traced back as specifically an American phenomenon, the spirit of irritability in concretising the issue onto an object of blame will, in its turn, arouse a curiosity followed quickly by an intellectual interest – or at least, a natural desire to learn more.

Discussion, motivated by anger and resentment, will evoke through an inevitable process, facts, figures, and reasons, in building arguments against the evils of globalisation and America as the advocate for its advance.   As David Hume argued long ago, reason and intellectual life stems from and remains the slave of our passions.   Whilst hatred may always be condemned as a thing in itself, on the other hand, its motivating power and that of anti-Americanism may be seen as a desirable influence in developing new areas of knowledge and uncovering the truth.   It will certainly act as a beneficial quality in demolishing a still widespread false consciousness of America as the "land of the free."

The virtue of an anti-American campaign may therefore be seen in its reinvigorating democratic political life throughout the globe through the popular concentration on the most relevant issues of our time. It may, indeed, be the *only* way of boosting successfully the spirit of democracy throughout the world, i.e. through simplifying and concretising issues which the majority find too complex or time-consuming to think out for themselves without the catalyst of a hate icon. It may be asked, is it unfair that the figure of America should be used in this way? The answer has to be No for the reasons given above, i.e. because of the *real* ills visited upon the world by American political intervention and financial power, and irrespective as to whether or not the majority of Americans are aware of the ills for which their country is directly responsible. Indeed, it is probable that the majority of Americans are unaware of the ills for which their country is responsible, and are no less ignorant of the workings and manifestations of globalisation than any other people in the world.

14 – Reservations with regard to anti-Americanism

This chapter cannot conclude without speculating as to how we should expect Americans to respond to such a campaign. As noted above, the campaign is aimed against the general or collective as opposed to the individual or specific, for the reason that the former is not only a substantive reality in its own right but is that which touches and affects the majority amongst the peoples of the world. That is, whilst American or Rentier capitalism may be injurious in its outcome, a particular individual capitalist may be the most amiable, gentle, and philanthropic person anywhere to be found. There is no suggestion that individual Americans are by nature selfish, mean, exploitative, or malicious, but only that the socio-economic framework within which they exist is so by the consequences of its system.

There is no suggestion in the campaign that we should be unfriendly or wish harm to individual Americans, and the author of this article, over many decades of personal contact, has usually found them most amiable, and has no reason for personal grudge against them in their singularity. My first contact with Americans was as a 7-year old evacuee in 1942 having sweets stuffed into my pockets by American soldiers on Swindon railway station, they having bought up huge tins of confectionary from the platform kiosk – luxuries usually denied Britons due to the unavailability of sufficient coupons in our Ration books. But such pleasant childhood memories – if it was a pleasant memory - should not be allowed to prejudice the adult mind in a world that has been transformed out of all recognition from that distant era. Although I do not recollect being alarmed by the episode, I do remember the GI exclaiming, "Don't be afraid, I'm only giving you some candies," or words to that effect, for I was unaccustomed to strange men thrusting their hands into my pockets.

Furthermore, as with most people, I am indebted to various bits of American technology, and have always been indebted to American research in different spheres of knowledge, and up to 45% of my specialised study material in the social sciences has either been printed in the USA or republished in this country. It should be noted that the best anti-globalisation literature comes out of America: the names of Noam Chomsky, David C. Korten (whom I have met personally), Joshua Karliner, and Hazel Henderson, are names of recent authors which immediately come to mind, without bothering to draw up a properly prioritised list of the most eminent. But technology and the world of academia does not typify the malign forces and influences which either oppress or damage the external world.

15 – The nastiness of the complacent

It has been noted here that the real problem of the Americans is their very niceness. This is because of their complacency, their optimism, and their Panglossian self-assurance that everything is right with the world. This was recently brought home to a friend with regular business contacts on a US bomber base. At a conference, shortly after the outbreak of the Iraqi War, she was appalled by the overwhelming benevolence and good humour of her hosts, as the champagne flowed and the salmon pâté was gratefully consumed, whilst thousands of Iraqis were losing their lives in a war zone – and losing them from bombs which were taking off from a runway only yards from the conference venue. Yet she was unable to confront her hosts or fault their perfect niceness.

All this brings to mind a delicious essay by Bertrand Russell on *Nice People*.[11] The essay opens with the words, "I intend to write an article in praise of nice people," and after eight pages of cutting observations on different aspects of human character, he concludes with the sentence, "In a word, nice people are those who have nasty minds." Self-righteousness is a very difficult thing to wrong-foot, but when it is part of the national psyche, as it is in America today, it is especially insidious. This is because it shuts the mind to self-criticism or doubt, and the Manicheism of George W. Bush with its categorising of the peoples of the world into Good and Evil (according to those who are "with us" or "against us") with no intervening greys, is not only vicious but tyrannical, absurd, simplistic, stupid, and contrary to all the facts of reality. It is an attitude which both solves nothing and explains nothing, and leaves people as pig-headed as they were before.

A typical example of the political self-righteousness of American attitudes by comparison with that of other peoples, was interestingly shown in a recent TV Panorama programme, shortly before the outbreak of the Iraqi War, between a group of New Yorkers seated in a soda fountain confronting the patrons of a Jordanian restaurant in Amman. Whilst the Americans, which included the City's ex-mayor, Ed Koch, were aggressively excitable and intent on point-scoring, the Jordanians (amongst whom must have been a fair proportion of Palestinians) were thoughtful, calmly objective in their response, and magnanimous in their attitude.

They were unprovoked by the hostility of the New Yorkers, and rather than falling into the trap of a verbal punch-

---

[11] Published in his book, *Why I am not a Christian & other Essays on Religion & Related Subjects*, Allen & Unwin, 1957.

up, they maintained their probity and good sense with informed and disinterested argument. Quite apart from the topic under discussion, it revealed the typical characteristics of two nationalities very different from one another: one, crude, uninformed, and narrow-minded, in a conflict situation; and the other, composed, cultured, intellectually well-endowed, and clearly nurtured in a society enjoying the benefits of an ancient civilisation.

16 – The fallacy of the chosen-people syndrome

It is astonishing to reflect that America has learned nothing from the horrific events of 9/11. Only a people with minds shut like a clam could be so myopic as never to have asked themselves the causes of 9/11. Has it never occurred to them that political desperation at the failure to effect change in a world of injustice, dispossession and tyranny led directly to the collapse of the World Trade Centre tower blocks? Has it not further occurred to them that continued deafness to the cries of oppression will lead inescapably to a madness of terrorism comparable to that experienced in the Israel of Ariel Sharon's Likud Party?

Are the Americans to proclaim themselves as the second of God's Chosen people, and hence the infallibility of their cause, and to take the consequences? In this world there are no Chosen people! When all false consciousness falls away, and all demand their rights, then all are equal. But if some choose nonetheless to elbow others aside, or to deny them their rights, as George W. Bush or Ariel Sharon – or even Tony Blair (grateful to walk in the footsteps of the powerful) – they may call upon their countries unending acts of terrorism and horrific suffering. This is because history and human nature has always demonstrated that the downtrodden never finally surrender to the will of their persecutors. These are the lessons which if America fails to learn through persuasion will eventually be enforced through the tragedy of experience.

The kindest gesture we can offer the American individual is the candour of confronting him (or her) with the iniquitous results of American power in its several aspects, and talking through the issues in the calm light of reason. The educated American from New York or New England (which produced a glorious flowering of literature in the 19th century), or from the enlightened state of California, may already have a sympathetic understanding of the issues raised in this book. Those sufficiently disinterested or well-travelled to break away from the provincialism of a small town milieu in priding themselves as world citizens rather than merely as nationals of a superpower, are very welcome to support this cause in recognition of their enlightenment. Those, too, who believe in a family of equal nations under the auspices of the UN are also welcome to join and support the laudable aims of this appeal.

17 – The poison of American-style religiosity

But those from the Bible belt and the Southern states, whose hearts have been hardened by the Old Testament Pharisaism and cruelty of a life-denying religion are unlikely to see any attraction in the present campaign. When religion is used as a tool for flag-waving chauvinism and the glorification of a narrow-visioned inward-looking society, as it is in so much of America, there is little hope for the future of humanity – although that is not to suggest that all American pastors are the hypocritical bigots as so often portrayed by the world's media.

In the context of the present paper, it cannot be left unsaid that the most iniquitous aspect of contemporary American religiosity is to be found in its apocalyptic millennialism. If such religiosity was found in a primitive Polynesian tribe (and it would not) there would be little threat to humanity, but manifested as it is amongst the most powerful nation on earth, it offers a dire threat to all the peoples of the planet. It is especially regrettable that the President now holding office belongs to a church which preaches the blessings of a fast-approaching Armageddon, and the division of the ways for us all into either Heaven or Hell. Jonathan Clarke has argued that, "Societies that persuade themselves that the end is nigh are societies which tend to behave irrationally and to enter into armed conflict."[12]

The wickedness of such beliefs, and the even greater wickedness of their propagation, is to be found in a fatalism which if met by a catastrophe, irrespective of whether it be natural, such as a major volcanic irruption, or man-made, such as a nuclear accident, is the acceptance of such disaster as God-given and deserved. The consequences of such an attitude, and such a theology, cannot but be a weakening of the will to counter such disaster with intelligence and determination, and instead, to accept the final reckoning with a contrite but hopeful heart as the outcome of a sinful world at the hands of a "loving" God.   In such a religious environment, prayer will replace ingenuity; superstition will replace intelligence; and love for the hereafter will exceed that for the planet which gave birth to our material existence. In the prospect of such a dreadful scenario, the atheist alone should be raised to the status of the true God!

18 – A wake-up call to the American people

The purpose of this appeal is to act as a catalyst in changing American attitudes to herself and as a wake-up call to the American social conscience and ethical thinking in questioning the fallibility of her own institutions. If that were to succeed it would stand as the proudest achievement of this book.

But before that an effective appeal has to be launched in serving the first purpose in liberating the peoples of the world from the thrall of American domination. A programme of education and co-operation must be embarked upon amongst all peoples as diverse as those from London to Beijing; from Oslo to Valparaiso; from Moscow to Sydney; from Berne to Bangkok; from Taipei to Dublin; from Mexico City to Calcutta; from Cairo to Manila; from Lagos to Jakarta; from Istanbul to

---

[12]   Quoted by Will Hutton in an essay in, *Rethinking British Decline*, ed. By R. English & M. Kenny, Macmillan, 2000, p. 150.

Rio de Janeiro; and from Rome to Mogadishu. Through a spirit of international friendship, and research into better arrangements for more equitable commerce and financial investment amongst nations, means will be found for securing greater concord and stability in the future.

That achieved, in our eyes would there be any remaining world leadership role left for America? Yes, but it would not be concerned with dominating and influencing the day-to-day lives of peoples beyond their borders. America needs a world role, and to deprive her of the privilege would lead to unfortunate withdrawal symptoms. The proposed role calls for the continued use and further development of her military-industrial complex but not in a function which might at first be thought. The new and proper world leadership role of America, through the utilisation of her NASA research centre, would be for the identification and diverting of meteorites endangering planet earth; interplanetary exploration with colonisation in mind; and finally, after some hundreds of years of research into ways of transporting matter at a million times the speed of light, interstellar exploration in the search for suitable planets to populate our people and spread the benefits of culture and civilisation.

Of course America would be assisted in the task, in both labour-skills and financially, by the rest of the world, but there is no reason why she should not be assured her pre-eminence and respect by the rest of us in such a vital field of activity. She could maintain her own distinctive sense of superiority (if she so desired) whilst keeping her nose out of the world's internal affairs as she concentrated her sights and her energy on the noble pursuit of extra-terrestrial matters of benefit to us all.

✷✷

CHAPTER 3

AMERICA AND THE DEBASEMENT OF CULTURAL VALUES

"The fact is that the Americans are not a thoughtful people: they are too busy to stop and question their values."

Dean W.R. Inge (Marchant, *Wit & Wisdom of Dean Inge*, No. 217.)

1 – Interrelationship between Cultural and Political values

Cultural and political values are not only closely interrelated in the consciousness of a society but at any one point in time are also reflected in its behaviour and way of life. The one cannot be entirely separated from the other, and so in considering the political characteristics of a country in any depth it is also necessary to consider its national character in a broader context.

If we dislike the politics of America, therefore, it will generally be found that we also dislike those values and beliefs which underpin its culture. Americans enjoy the conviction that their country is the best and greatest in the world. The *real* reason for this conviction is that their's is the largest and most powerful country in the world, although few would choose to rationalise this as a valid justification of their assumed superiority. The *given* reason for this conviction is always that their country represents *freedom* and *democracy* in their most ideal and indeed, in their only acceptable forms, and that therefore they have an exclusive and god-given mission to replicate these values as they see them to the rest of humanity.

2 – Some difficulties in defining Freedom and Democracy

Now although the American comprehends the ideas of Freedom and Democracy in a clear and unambiguous light, the truth is that *their* understanding of this is in no sense obvious to others if seen from the perspective of objective sociological reality. If an attempt is made to define these concepts in a general or abstract sense, or from an individual's personal desires out of context with the broader needs of the community, the outcome is a superficial and entirely unsatisfactory understanding. For example, one man's freedom which imposes on that of another is no sound basis for a free society. Furthermore, mere arbitrary wish-fulfilment is no good foundation for freedom if such wishes prove harmful to their subjects – which they often do.

Hence a proper understanding of freedom and democracy cannot escape the necessity of considering such questions as what is good or bad for individuals and society. The benefits of freedom and democracy can only ultimately be assessed according to the type of society which emerges through the experience of these values. Any other criterion would be naïve, unreal, or reflect an impractical grasp of what these concepts really meant. If a bad society emerges from freedom and democracy, are we then to conclude that these values in themselves are bad? No, we are only to conclude that their concept of freedom was faulty, or that their mechanisms of government failed to carry through the demands of a democratic society.

American democracy may be faulted from many points of view, but there is one overriding critical observation to which all others must be subordinated. American democracy arose from a particular type of popular culture and mindset which has never existed in any previous society. Popular cultural forms and mindsets have often emerged in the post-industrial era but, predominantly, they remained particular to specific classes or population sectors. In the non-American world, such popular cultures were usually found amongst the poorer or more depressed levels of the community. Such cultures tended to be disparaged by the middle or more privileged sectors of society, not necessarily on account of their specific characteristics, but more significantly because they reflected a lower level of consciousness or understanding of those values contributing to human progress. There was a universal awareness that such cultures lacked depth of meaning as a guide towards better attitudes, taste, and forms of living.

In America, on the other hand, the popular culture which arose in the post-industrial age differed in one respect from that of all other peoples, with widespread consequences which could never have been anticipated. It was not particular to a specific class or population sector, but was universal across the entire spectrum of society. It was accepted and disseminated as part of the national democratic consciousness of the people, not through the natural values of a moral sense or education, but through the power of marketing or the influence of the almighty dollar.

As the existence of a popular culture by its definition, imposes a ceiling on its own potential in terms of depth of understanding or value, and since it is universal and equal in its appeal across all sectors of society, the inevitable outcome is a general depression of standards on all those spheres of life touching on thought, life-styles, leisure, and the arts. As Elbert Hubbard has argued, "This will never be a civilised country until we expend more money for books than we do for chewing-gum."[13]   Even that infinitesimal minority representing the intellectual elite has not escaped entirely from this poison. The implication of this populist culture, and its malign impact on political life, will only become fully apparent in the arguments laid out in this chapter and the following.

American democracy has therefore arisen in an inauspicious environment, whereby it was hobbled from the beginning. It emerged from a state of mind which demands that standards for thinking and action in the common sphere of life should be reduced from a higher to a lower level. It demands a debasing populism which is demeaning to the better nature and aptitudes of the individual. The outcome is a coarsening of human nature; an over-emphasis on action and a trivialising of thought; a vulgarity of manners and a knockabout humour. All these attitudes are a direct expression of the American democratic spirit, and in all these manifestations Americans take

---

[13]   Elbert Hubbard, *The Philistine*, Vol. XXV, p. 1.

a pride, conscious of the fact that it separates them from all other peoples on the planet. In the words of H.V. Miller, "it is the American vice, the democratic disease which expresses its tyranny by reducing everything unique to the level of the herd."[14]

3 – Americans subject to a universal dislike

The more remarkable fact is that peoples across the globe, of the most diverse cultures and political systems recognise the above characteristics as distinctively and uniquely American. Furthermore, the peoples of the world disdain these characteristics, and cannot refrain from mocking and sneering at them, for reasons which are universally understood.

The common opinion is that Americans are not merely objectionable due to superficial appearances, but that they uphold and cherish false values. Is America wrong and the rest of the world right, or vice versa? Has America perchance invented a new social consciousness which transcends the values of the Old World? These questions must be addressed, and they can only be answered by examining closely a number of substantive issues impacting on the good and bad of human societies.

The real fear of thinking peoples throughout the world is that American power exerts a malign influence on their native cultures. If Americans wish to live in a society where standards of taste are reduced to the lowest common denomination of understanding, then that is their right. Every people must maintain its own cultural integrity. But no country has the right to enforce its standards on other peoples – and that is the effect of America, not so much politically, as through the ubiquity of her cultural media and transnational corporations.

---

[14] H.V. Miller, On Democracy, *The Wisdom of The Heart*, 1947.

4 – Problems of debasing cultural values

But more objectionable is the ideological belief of Americans that the reduction of standards to supposedly suit the mindset and understanding of the simplest individuals follows as a natural attribute of the democratic spirit. To resist or oppose the demands of populism is mistakenly interpreted as undemocratic and elitist. Americans see themselves in this light as the benefactors of the world; whilst thinking people, on the contrary, see this as a gesture of contempt by a foreign power, not simply because it is symptomatic of a clash of cultures, but actually undermines the cultural integrity of peoples. The attitude of Americans in this context is regarded as an outrage. Nothing so much unites the peoples of the world as the commonly held perception of what America is.

What most divides the mentality of America from the rest of the world is that the peoples in the latter – particularly amongst the more advanced cultures – believe in the possibility for the infinite aspirations of the individual and society and that *nothing can or should act as a mediating influence in frustrating* the on-going struggle for the achievement of those aspirations, and a debasing populism clearly acts as a mediating influence in frustrating progress. In the non-American world there may still exist societies which are stratified by privilege, caste, class-consciousness, intolerance, or tyranny, but in the 21st century these abuses are readily recognised as such, and there is general agreement to end them.

But despite this, in the non-American world the concept of justice and egalitarianism insists that no ceiling should be put on standards which frustrate the achievement of the free individual, and that the concept of standards for achievement is something which is fixed and unalterable, and not negotiable to suit one person rather than another. All individuals in society – all humanity – should be equally placed with regard to ideal standards in every aspect of life. A truly free and democratic society demands that aspirations for achievement and standards are always non-negotiable and just as they cannot be altered to suit one individual rather than another, so in the same way they cannot be altered to suit one class rather than another. This is because deferment to ignorance, or those with an undeveloped understanding, or those who are insufficiently educated, is not merely patronising, but seemingly acknowledges unbridgeable levels of understanding as a basis for class privilege.

And in the sphere of democratic politics, with regard to identifying and discussing means and ends, such a situation contradicts the principles of equality necessary in facilitating the practical purpose of democracy. Democracy is a process through which the equality of all should have an opportunity to express, not merely the superficiality of arbitrary caprice, but rather rational choice which assists in the development of full potential. But the achievement of the latter is only possible if debasing populism is eschewed in favour of a higher understanding which allows for such rational choice.

5 – Comparison between American and non-American values

The consequence of this cultural outlook in the non-American world is that those at the apex of society are perceived as enjoying the best standards in society, and if they are also those of goodwill, they are also perceived as representing the ideal good in society, and this makes them worthy of emulation. Hence the humble or middling majority, those from the peasant to the newly-affluent, would prefer if they could be re-born into another life, to be re-created as the sons or daughters of those at the apex of society. Such yearnings need not necessarily reflect a desire to greater wealth or financial security, or even for status, but rather a desire to enjoy all that is perceived as best in the culture of that society. These attitudes are universal throughout the non-American world as somehow reflecting the reality of existence.

Now the general world outlook of Americans is quite different from this, and consequently, it has turned them into a people which are uniquely separate from the rest of humanity.

The American individual asserts that he is as good as anyone else in society, and the assertion is not made as a rhetorical claim for rights as such a statement would be interpreted if made by someone in the non-American world, but as a conviction that he is *actually* equal to anyone else in society. Now such a claim in the non-American world would be dismissed as an absurdity and plain untruth. On what basis can any individual claim to be as good as or as equal with anyone else in the community in any real sense? Such an assumption is based on an illusion. Such a conviction may inflate the ego and self-confidence, and go far in creating an exaggerated assertiveness. It will eventually give rise to an objectionable personality, and a mindset which defies the facts of reality.

The responsibility for this mindset, of course, is traceable to the ideology of American democratic life. The core of this ideology is to be found in a particular type of populism which repudiates all hierarchical authority as an infringement on freedom. As all hierarchies were condemned as tyranny, the individual was forced to look into himself for the end-good of society, and this in turn led to the fragmentation of the idea for the rational organisation of society except as mediated through the immediate material desires of the individual. And through this emerged the pioneering spirit which offered a practical framework for the idea of nationhood in an empty landmass offering opportunities for infinite expansion and movement towards the West.

6 – Origin of American values

It was the conjunction of all these factors which alone enabled the development of the American outlook, but the strength of feeling and convictions which arose can only be understood in their historical context. The ancestry of America is comprised of minorities which clashed with established authority; who separated – or were already separated from the main body of society; and who fled from persecution or oppression. If Englishmen arrived in New England in the early

17th century with their noses slit or their ears lopped off because they refused to accept the tenets or ritual of the established church; or Frenchmen arrived towards the end of the same century because the legal rights established a hundred years earlier upholding their religious practices had suddenly been revoked; or the Irish arrived because of poverty and the potato famine in the 1840s as the British government failed to authorise simple trading measures to relieve these evils; or Jews arrived from Russia at the turn of the 19th and 20th centuries because their villages were arbitrarily set aflame, and they were cut down by the sabres of the Tsarist police; or Armenians arrived from Anatolia in the 1890s or after 1915 because of Turkish inflicted massacres, these things left a lasting mark on the psyche of American people which was not easily to be erased through the passing of the generations.

Americans developed a hatred and contempt for the Old world because of the injustice it inflicted on their ancestors; and eventually this hatred was transmuted into a sense of national superiority and overweening pride and an inclination to ridicule peoples beyond their frontiers. It became natural to argue that nothing was worse than the Old world and that nothing was better than the New. But it should be borne in mind that those who fled from the Old world were not representative of majorities, and this twice divided them from their nations of old: firstly, in that they were anyway minorities; and secondly, in that a self-imposed exile and their absorption in the New world distanced them further from the soil from whence they came.

The majority of immigrants not only turned their backs forever on the Old world but strove to forget the past in looking forward to a new future. In cutting the umbilical cord they chose to regard the past as irrelevant and too painful for recollection. To look back would undermine confidence and feelings of self-esteem in meeting the challenges ahead. With the passing of the generations these feelings turned to a disinterest in understanding the political complexities of their countries of origin, until their concepts of them became a parody or a stereotypical set of bad impressions.

7 – Their disparaging of the strange and foreign

These impressions were strengthened as Americans became more isolated and introverted within their vast continent, until they took a strangely perverted pride in their ignorance of the outside world. This strangely exuberant ignorance of the non-American world is most typically expressed in Mark Twain's, *The Innocents Abroad*, a travel book which glorifies the ignorance of the author in confronting the exotic, the fantastical, the outlandish, the comical, and the shocking, in the Europe and Near East of the 1870s, whilst failing to grasp the real meaning of anything.

It is a book which confirms all the long-held prejudices of the American people – and was written for just such a purpose – viz., that Europe or the wider world, has nothing to offer which makes sense to the purpose of American life. Europe is to be seen as nothing more than a zoo filled with exotic animals which are to be laughed at for their strange antics as one passes from one cage to another. As they are beyond understanding there is nothing more to describe than the visual and superficial impact they make on the senses. It was as if non-American humanity belonged to another planet. These dismissive attitudes which are only disrespectful because Americans have no time or patience to comprehend the essence of reality or the meaning of things, are reflected in a thousand Hollywood movies over the past century, or as reflected on the wider canvas of journalism and literature, as well as in the behaviour and manners of Americans with whom many of us are brought into contact.

I well remember the first occasion I was brought into contact with the disrespectful gesture of Americans towards a foreign power – even when supposedly it was an ally. As a nine-year old during the War in 1944 I was taken by the matron of my boarding school in a taxi to a nearby hospital for specialist treatment, when the driver observed that lipstick had been put on the statue of Queen Victoria in the market square. The matron, who at the best of times was a dyspeptic and irritable old woman, responded with a sneer, "It's those

Americans again! They've never had respect for our imperial past." The remark may sound comically anachronistic in today's world, but it nonetheless reflected a justifiable resentment at the time.

The development of such attitudes, with its ready humour to disparage all that is strange or foreign, would not have been possible without the growth of a mindset and ideology which separated humanity into two contrasting groups. The repudiation of the idea of hierarchy as entailing inevitably and always the tyranny of an elite over the majority, conjured into existence a populist concept of freedom and democracy which idealised the common norm of standards as against the idea of the best. Consequently, the idea of striving for quality as a universal standard was regarded with suspicion as elitist and somehow threatening the democratic spirit.

Therefore, in addressing the needs of the majority a dumbed-down or downwardly-aspiring approach needed to be adopted. This called for the compromising of standards to fit the norms of the below average common man or woman. This was justified on the grounds that what could not be comprehended by the poorly-educated majority was not only unworthy of popular interest but its attempted presentation amounted to an encroachment on the self-esteem and dignity of that majority. To go "above the head" of the majority, intentionally or otherwise, was not only considered "bad form" but was actually interpreted as undemocratic or as some kind of Old world aristocratic pretentiousness which needed to be burst by the pin-prick of humour.

8 – The proletarianisation of society

The consequence of these thought patterns brought into existence the need for the proletarianisation of society – not in the Marxist sense of a class consciousness prepared for class war, but in a universal sense in that humanity, in safeguarding democracy, should be reduced to the level of a simplistic populist culture from which none should be excluded through want of exerting their mental powers, or lack of vision or percipience. This was to be a happy-clappy society of smiling exuberant nerds, acquisitive of ever-more useless baubles in warding off discontent in lieu of any other inclination for self-fulfilment; of masses so superficial in their approach to life, that they intentionally cultivated a mindlessness through constant and frenetic movement as they passed from one activity to another. What unified society was the simplistic undefined notion that all were free, linked to the assertion that that which was incomprehensible to the least intelligent was not merely insignificant as a social fact but was actually at enmity with the popular will.

None of these notions were systematically formulated as the basis for democratic ideology – although the Philosophical Pragmatists (a uniquely American school of thinking) came close to such conclusions. These notions arose spontaneously through the evolution of American society and are made evident through historical fact, and in that is to be found the sheer horror of the situation. A synthetically formulated ideology, such as Soviet Communism, remains always a vulnerable phenomenon, since it exists within the framework of a political system, and as soon as the regime falls, so too will its ideology melt away like a snowfall on a spring morn. But an ideology or world outlook emerging through natural as contrasted with politically-planned development is more deeply-felt and long-lasting since it defines the national character of a people. And this is the situation with America in underlining its real threat to the world.

It is not simply the organisation of a political system which threatens to overwhelm the globe, but an ideology deeply embedded in the national psyche. Americans hold political and other convictions which are taught in their schools and fundamentalist churches, but if these things had never been taught in a formal setting, it is probable they would nonetheless be held with hardly less conviction. This is because the influences of family and social life are sufficient to create and enforce the majority of prejudices, and this further demonstrates the implacability of the cultural and political threat.

The debasement of culture within America is marked by a general attitude which imposes the necessity for reducing standards to the common norm as a democratic gesture to the feelings of the majority, but this is not to suggest that America is without cultural institutions, orchestras, galleries, etc., which meet the highest of world standards. Examples can be cited of cultural predominance not found elsewhere in the world: for example, the Metropolitan Opera in New York is the only remaining theatre where decent stage productions of Wagner's *Ring* are still performed.[15] America has many of the world's greatest singers, artists, writers and socio-political scientists, but none of these positive attributes are sufficient to make a significant impact on the general philistinism of American life or to reduce the effect of this worldwide.

9 – The movement to dumb-down culture

A conscious move by leading opinion-formers to proletarianise or dumb-down American culture is traceable to the last quarter of the 19th century. This arose through a cultural conflict within the middle class itself. It was initiated by the question of how to respond to the influx of vast numbers of ignorant and barely literate immigrants from the Old world: should they be absorbed through education in adopting accepted standards of thinking, behaviour, and taste, or was it necessary for the established population to compromise their own position by stooping to the level of this new proletariat?

Alarmed at the increasing vulgarisation of American society, a group of prominent writers and magazine editors, led by Harvard art history professor Charles Eliot Norton, and New York Editors, Richard Watson Gilder of, *The Century* magazine, and E.L. Godkin of, *The Nation*, set out to reverse the trend by attempting to codify Victorian standards for literature and the fine arts. Together with the support of artistic allies in Boston and New York, they launched a campaign to improve American

---

[15] Following a recent review by Michael Portillo in the *New Statesman*, it is apparent that the Seattle Opera may be added to that of the Metropolitan.

taste in interior furnishings, textiles, ceramics, wallpapaer, and books. In this way they hoped to achieve a coherent national artistic culture. Godkin wrote despairingly about what he described as the "chromo civilisation" of trashy books and garish chromolithographic prints, and together with Norton and Gilder, and editors of other quality journals such as, the *Atlantic Monthly* (which published all the works of Henry James) and the *North American Review*, they established new guidelines for serious literature.

But this movement soon came under attack, as "elitist" and attempting to impose an "imperialistic control over the nation's literary standards." Mark Twain was in the forefront of the attack, when he mustered together the younger generation of writers, and declared in his strident style, that he was through with "literature and all that bosh." He attacked the aristocratic literary conventions, and in competing with the quality journals retailing at 35 cents, new magazines as the *Ladies Journal*, *Cosmopolitan*, and *McClure's* lowered their prices to 15 cents, and through the support of advertising rather than subscriptions, tripled or quadrupled their circulation.

This was the beginning of the slippery slope into the worst kind of populism, when the subjectivity of marketing, as opposed to the objective appeal of quality, became the criterion in deciding sales' success. And in the sphere of authorship, Mark Twain became the first writer to consciously turn himself into a media personality, through founding his own publishing house, adopting a distinctive appearance, selling his books through door-to-door salesmen, and lecturing coast to coast.

No criticism is intended here of Mark Twain or his writings, and neither are we criticising the literary movement of which he was a leader. The process of all history entails the rebounding of opposites against one another, and in all are to be found objective grounds for pro and contra. The purpose of the above, is merely to point out that in this particular cultural clash, it was the populists who prevailed over the advocates for artistic merit, and that in the longer term this has proved unfortunate for the fate of American culture.

10 – Examples of American mass culture

Populist American culture – and all that is truly American – has since the mid 19th century therefore derived its inspiration from the lowest echelons of society, especially with regard to manners, music, and much of fiction. This is not to denigrate those art forms at the base of society, for all artistic media, irrespective of its origin, is as equally worthy of consideration and study as that emanating from the apex of society. But when culture, manners, or thought patterns from the base of the community, influence the general direction of a people, this in itself raises a host of other issues. The question is often raised: is this symptomatic of decadence? Arnold Toynbee in his magnum opus, *A Study of History*, certainly thought so, and he argues from his in-depth study of 23 civilisations, that the imitation of those at the base of society, or when proletariats inspire those at higher levels in the hierarchy, is always a symptom of degeneracy.

What, then, are to conclude from the two startling modes of walking common amongst all sectors of American society, and not found in any part of Europe or the Far East? Firstly, there is the slovenly hip-swinging walk in imitation of the black slave population and it certainly does not contribute to a favourable impression of a people with pretensions to world leadership. Such a style of walking may be of little concern to the majority but it is objectionable to non-Americans with a military background since it seems to contradict the ethos of disciplined service life.

Secondly, there is the ape-like walk in imitation of circus chimpanzees, adopted as a boastful stance, and sometimes to express aggression. Note, especially, when cowboys walk towards one another, their hands in readiness to draw their guns. Likewise, Europeans and peoples of the Far East are often taken aback by the lazily off-hand manners of American military personnel to one another between the ranks: e.g., the offensive familiarity of officers to men is hardly designed to gain respect, as is also the failure of other ranks to stand to attention when addressed by superiors. The idea of such an undisciplined horde is hardly likely to win the confidence of the world in the struggle for a better future.

Amongst the worst aspects of American culture with regard to its propagation in the non-American world is the ubiquitous influence of the Hollywood film; and through powerful commercial franchises, malign changes to eating habits. The Hollywood film may be denigrated on three counts: firstly, because of the low standard in film making in appealing to the lowest common denominator in maximising box office receipts; secondly, in propagating false and demeaning attitudes and manners; and thirdly, in actually encouraging violence and criminal activity amongst those inclined to law-breaking.

It is ironic that one of the greatest art forms of modern times should be turned by Hollywood into a mere production-line industry with little artistic merit, and then enforced upon the rest of the world through the vested interests of stockholders, so that the non-American film is pushed to the margins of existence. This depressing situation is only alleviated by the hope that the invention and marketing of the DVD, and the home-study which this medium provides, offers the promise that future generations may be alerted to the truly great cinema of countries which hitherto have been put into the shade, such as Sweden, Japan, France, China, Italy, Russia, etc.

Turning to the American cartoon film, and its influence on very young children, nothing has been so designed which encourages misbehaviour, bad manners, the mocking of disability,[16] or even violent attitudes. The American cartoon, as indeed with adult films, has been designed to maximise box office receipts, and with this in mind, directors have sought with subtlety to exploit the hidden cruelty and moral failings often found amongst the very young. It is difficult to imagine financial gain put to a more wicked purpose. A comparison with the cartoon film industries of any non-American country soon demonstrates a remarkable contrast between art forms used for good or ill intent.

---

[16] I have especially in mind the *Mr. Magoo* cartoons which make fun of short-sightedness.

The obesity crisis throughout the developed world is accountable directly to transnational American food corporations and their cultivation of fast-food habits together with the consumption of unhealthy high-fat diets in preference to fresh fruit and vegetables. Even if such chains as Macdonalds, KFC, and Starbucks, are not wholly responsible for obesity, their widespread sales publicity through the media (especially when aimed at children) in conjunction with their impact in influencing locally-owned business to follow in their tracks, is certainly evidence of a widespread effect in encouraging a snack culture and the demise of traditional family dining.

It has been argued that all international retail corporations are undesirable in promoting the bland standardisation of dubious products, but this needs to be qualified. There is a sharp divide between the products and services of American corporations, and those of all other countries. As the American is primarily interested in maximising shareholders' profits he has little interest in consumers' benefit, and consequently, his products and services are generally shoddy or indifferent. Whilst American food products are tasteless and even life-threatening, their IT and technical merchandise approaches the most unreliable in the world, only that of the old East bloc being of a worse quality. In America there is little consumer protection, and American industrialists in contrast to those in the rest of the world, are too ruthless in their grasping after profits to have much sense of obligation towards those who dare become their customers.

11 – A dumbed-down culture unique to America

The above critique of American democratic culture and its adverse impact on humanity in lowering all standards apart from those affecting certain aspects of material comfort, can only be understood in its sharpest light in the context of comparison with the rest of the world. It is often suggested that America is no more than the expression of an inescapable modernism in the contemporary world, and that hence Americanism is an inevitable fact of life. But this view is false. The one does not follow from the other simply as a consequence of evolutionary progress.

America is unique and separate from all other peoples and cultures, and what is attributed as American in the non-American world is accountable directly to the financial-industrial power of that single nation. The fact that America was able to enforce her products or styles of living on other countries may be evidence that the latter were ripe to receive them, but it does not follow that they would have appeared there spontaneously as home-grown products if America had never existed.

For example, no other country on earth has ever developed a dumbed-down culture or sought to reduce or compress standards to suit the common norm of the below average individual – at least not intentionally. Not even Communism, during the worst excesses of Soviet rule, attempted to proletarianise its population as America succeeded in doing from early in its history. Although the Soviets created an ideology out of the proletariat it was more pastiche than reality, for privilege and hero-worship of selected categories of individuals soon saw the creation of an inegalitarian society with its own aristocracy of party members.

Furthermore, American popular music was soon seized upon and condemned as decadent, not because it was proletarian (which in truth it was) but because its anarchic rebelliousness threatened the idea of social cohesion and the will to struggle towards the ever-higher uplands of social progress. American music, as with the rest of its culture, represented everything which was undesirable. Meanwhile, no expense was spared by the countries of the Soviet bloc in staging the most elaborate and costly productions of classical opera and ballet in meeting the highest standards of realism and drama.

Taking culture in its broadest sense, to include the arts, life-style, clothing, catering arrangements, and manners, etc., the idea and practice that this should be designed for a below average mass of humanity is specific to America alone. European and other peoples may always have had popular art forms, particularly with regard to music or the dance, but these things were accepted and enjoyed by all society, and carried no stigma of a dumbed-down culture. The stigma attached to American culture is the imperative for technical simplicity so that nothing is allowed to confound the sense or intelligence of the below average majority.

When American popular culture reached Europe or other sophisticated societies as Japan, it was at first interpreted as degrading to society in attempting to appeal to the least skilled and poorest sectors of the community. This, of course, was never the intention of American culture in its homeland where it was accepted universally in expressing the anarchic spirit of the country. But as soon as the culture was transferred to a foreign clime it was seen in quite another light.

In the non-American world mainline culture has always been projected as offering a universal appeal. It has seldom been suspect as patronising lower level taste or intelligence, and has seldom compromised its integrity to its artistic or other purpose – i.e. not until the onslaught of America on the world. Until the last quarter of the 19th century the working class man in Britain or on the Continent read and absorbed newspapers, journals and pamphlets which were typeset and written in a journalistic or literary style differing little from those of the middle or upper classes. Hence there was a closer intellectual link within society which offered a better medium for understanding between contrasting sectors of the community.

This unity was broken with the advent of populist American-inspired tabloids, some established and led by press moguls from the north American continent such as Lords Beaverbrook and Thomson. Such men founded a gutter press which in true American fashion appealed to the worst feelings and prejudices of ill-educated people and manipulated them for an ulterior political purpose. This new simplistic and often vicious journalism set-back the social consciousness and educational standards of the majority by a hundred years. This type of journalism was much slower in reaching the Continent, and until this day remains almost negligible in the Scandinavian countries where high standards are consistently maintained.

12 – Emergence of a hedonistic youth culture

But these subtle penetrations of American culture into the European way of life were not recognised at the time for the degenerate forces they were. Consequently, they played little part in arousing anti-American feeling. But the youth culture certainly did. Although today we accept youth culture as a part of natural existence, in origin it is specifically American, and has not arisen as a spontaneous phenomenon within the culture of any other people. This brings to mind Oscar Wilde's quip that "the youth of America is their oldest tradition. It has been going on now for three hundred years."[17] Of course there have always been rebellious groups amongst the young expressing new ideas in the evolution towards greater progress, especially within student circles, and these expressed the inevitable conflict between the generations.

But the youth culture phenomenon which leapt out of America to infect the world was something different, since it had no pretensions to propagating new ideas or advancing progress. It was and has always remained a mere sub-culture for promoting leisure or hedonistic values for their own sake. It may be asked, what was the purpose of a youth culture? What social benefits did it set out to achieve? The answer is none. It simply emerged spontaneously from the nihilistic aspects of American life. The interesting fact to observe is that not only is there no need for a youth culture, but that its existence acts as a deviation from the ongoing development between childhood and maturity. It transports the teenager away from childhood but instead of directing him onto the path of adulthood, it blocks his natural development by taking him on a meaningless journey which fails to prepare him for the future. His time is wasted in useless and sometimes harmful pursuits.

---

[17] Oscar Wilde, *A Woman of No Importance*, Act I.

In a world pre-dating the existence of youth culture, it may be asked, was there any latent demand for such a culture by the young themselves? The answer has to be No. The very concept of a youth culture intervening as an interruption between childhood and maturity is not only patronising but demeaning. The normal child – unless he is a Peter Pan – strives towards adulthood as soon as it may be achieved. He looks forward towards equality with grown-ups and sharing their privileges and enjoyments.

Why should the achievement of this be frustrated by a youth culture? In a healthy well-balanced society – and certainly in a well-mannered society – there is always an attempt to mix the generations in any social context. The older generations, if they want their children or grandchildren to follow their example and be influenced by their values, encourage their children of, from say, five onwards to mix with their elders at family and other social gatherings, for how otherwise can the young be absorbed successfully into the mainstream culture of society? Do children themselves want to be excluded from the company of their elders? The answer is No.

13 – Early response to youth culture in Europe

Then how did the *idea* for a youth culture first come into consciousness? As with so many things American, the answer is that it was invented as a marketing ploy. There is money to be made from young people, and since they are young, they are that more gullible than their elders, and hence in the eyes of American marketing moguls, they are ideal material for exploitation. The distinctive mark of American business is that it is usually unscrupulous and often immoral. Furthermore, the American business mind has a genius for inventing products and services which are short-lived and surplus to necessity, and then selling them worldwide with remarkable success.

Whilst in the non-American world the value of a thing is judged by its utility, in the world of American business the only justification for a product or service is the return it brings to shareholders. Consequently, American corporations invested heavily in the youth culture, not only in the sphere of popular music, but in clothing, in trade marking or franchising popular cartoon characters on an infinite variety of household or personal products from tooth brushes to porridge bowls, and in the production of never-ending gewgaws of ephemeral appeal, and eventually, the marketing of drugs to the young through established criminal networks.

As the American youth culture did not penetrate Europe until the late 1940s and early 1950s, I am old enough to remember a world without pop music, youth fashions, drugs, etc., and their accompanying lifestyles. When the youth culture first hit Europe it was seen as designed for and appealing to the working class only, and consequently, middle class parents were appalled by everything it represented in depressing cultural standards. Hence the same misinterpretation of youth culture was made by non-Americans everywhere as had been made in interpreting the broader aspects of American popular culture, viz., that it was designed for the lower echelons of society. But in the eyes of Americans this was not the case, for the youth culture was intended to have a universal appeal, and this was something which Europeans just could not comprehend.

How could educated people be expected to waste their time with jazz or pop music, so the argument ran, in a world of Mozart, Verdi, or Mahler? At school we listened to classical music because there *was* no alternative, apart from the accepted popular music of big band dance orchestras, palm court ensembles, or current tunes and songs enjoyed by young and old alike across the spectrum of society. In the early 50s I used to holiday at the home of an elderly aunt and grandmother who employed a West German au pair who explained that her parents and others in her social circle forbad their children tuning into AFN Frankfurt or otherwise listening to jazz or other American music which they regarded as "degenerate" and "preventing" the development of good character. *Ordentlich* (respectable) people just did not listen to American music!

Meanwhile in London my younger brother was actually expelled from the parental home at the age of 16 for playing jazz on his trumpet and dressing and generally behaving in a manner which was not expected of him, and this was followed up with a police injunction preventing him from entering the home when my parents were away at their seaside villa. I was warned by my father not to associate with my brother, since he had thrown away his chances of benefiting from a decent education, and was destined for a life of misery, poverty, and crime.[18] I only cite these stories since they illustrate the shocked response of an older generation to the impact of American youth culture on their susceptibilities.

14 – America and the drug culture

The correlative of the popular music of the American youth culture has always been drugs, and again, the origin of the drug culture and its propagation worldwide is exclusively American. Wherever Americans are gathered in any number there also will usually be drugs, and at private social events there is often on offer cocaine and heroin, and a choice of other narcotics. It was Americans through the pseudo-criminal fraternity who first established and still run the worldwide network of drug marketing and sales. I use the term pseudo since the criminal fraternity work in close association with the police, judges, local government officers, and elected representatives, etc., all of whom are on their payroll, and so an illegal activity has bought its own legality and become absorbed within the establishment.[19] Again, the growth of the drugs industry and its development into a culture did not become a worldwide phenomenon until the post-War period.

In the Western world a drug culture had never existed before, and because of its source, the death of every child, or son

---

[18] The fact that he eventually became a teacher and headmaster is another story. Parental discipline did not take effect for in his late 60s he is still playing jazz on his trumpet with groups in clubs and bars, usually to the applause of his own generation.

[19] There are many scholarly works tracing the history of the American drugs industry, but for an easily accessible account, the three *Godfather* films are worth viewing, since they are based on fact and do trace those significant landmarks in the post-War period.

or daughter, brother or sister, from drug abuse may with some justification be blamed on the unpardonable power of American financial trading. Despite this, however, the probability should be pointed out that as many people died of drug abuse in the 19th century as die today, but the significant difference is that in the earlier period these deaths arose from the abuse of drugs through medication, either prescribed or over the counter, and not through cultivated leisure use. What originated in the 19th century as a painkiller soon became an addiction or a secret vice.

For example, Thomas de Quincy became an opium eater through an apothecary's remedy for toothache, and every reader of Conan Doyle knows that Sherlock Holmes occasionally snorted cocaine, a habit frowned upon by his friend and colleague Dr. Watson. A culture of drug taking is more dangerous than risks exposed to medication, and for this reason efforts should generally be made to repel the American presence in the spheres of both business and social life. These things go far in explaining the depth of worldwide anti-American feeling.

The drug culture was launched on the world through the manifestations of the American youth culture in the late 1940s and 50s, but its full force did not take effect until the 1960s. In demonstrating the significance of this, my generation which experienced its teenage years in the late 40s and 50s, was hardly touched by the drug culture, and I can say that I have never personally known anyone who became addicted to or even experimented with drugs. On only one occasion have I have been offered drugs and that was by a middle aged man with whom I shared a cabin on the ferry crossing on the Hook to Harwich in the 1990s. He offered me a cannabis cigarette which I politely declined on the grounds that I was driving.

15 – Art forms and their influence on character

The panic of parents throughout Europe in the immediate post-War period in response to the cultural invasion by America may, in some respects, appear alarmist and absurd to the majority living today. What harm, it may be asked, was there ever in jazz? Today its enthusiasts belong predominantly to a staid and elderly generation – usually respectable, even conservative in their outlook, typified perhaps, by the ex-Tory minister, Kenneth Clarke, whose talks on the joys of jazz is a much-appreciated regular feature on BBC Radio 4. What harm, it may be asked, is there in Rock and Roll, or bepop, heavy metal, or any other form of pop music? This raises the entire question of art and its direct influence on attitudes and behaviour.

Leaving aside literary art forms, since they may be explicit or unambiguous in the expression of meaning or in directing the behaviour of readers, little blame can be attributed directly to music, painting, or the plastic arts *per se* in influencing thought or action. These latter art forms do influence behaviour but only within a wider cultural context. For example, Christian art, such as music and painting within a place of worship, certainly serves to stimulate the religious instinct, and this fact has always been recognised, but such art may be removed from its subjective context and appreciated objectively for its aesthetic qualities by those of any religion or none or by those of any culture. Those in the West who adorn their houses with Buddhas or Hindu deities are rarely supporters of those faiths.

Turning to music, the most abstract of the arts, its influence in stirring emotions and thought for good or ill has been recognised since the time of Plato and before. The Greeks placed music as a leading subject on the educational curriculum, since they connected it with so many other aspects of life and learning, e.g., poetry, drama, and mathematics, and Plato discusses in considerable depth the psychological relationship of music to the *spirit* (most notably in the *Republic* and the *Laws*) and its good and bad influence on character, both according to the type of music played and frequency of listening. His arguments still stand as fresh and valid to this day. Nonetheless, a discussion of the good or bad influence of music on attitudes and behaviour can only be intelligently undertaken within a wider socio-cultural context.

Whilst the differing forms of pop music may be simplistic in style and appeal, and usually marked by a heavy and repetitious beat, this in itself should not be used a critique of the art form *per se*. It is only if such music tends to attract a certain following, or flourishes for some inexplicable reason within a certain milieu, which is mindless, destructively hedonistic, closely associated with a drugs culture, or is otherwise anti-social or even criminal, that the question arises as to the social consequences of such music. The fact that such music is not *intrinsically harmful* as a social influence (as could be the case with a literary medium such as a vicious pamphlet) is clearly demonstrated by the realisation that it is time-circumscribed with regard to its social significance. That is, pop music after a duration of 50 years or so, becomes established as a historical relict: of little interest to the younger generation, but of some interest as quaint in arousing sentimental thoughts about the past in the older generations. Such music, therefore, loses the social power which it once had and becomes banal or meaningless to the majority of a later era.

These factors, therefore, give some justification to the alarm experienced by our parents, grandparents, or even great-grandparents of the immediate post-War era to the anti-social manifestations of the American cultural onslaught – although it can never justify the cruelty they may have inflicted on their children. This is because within a certain time-frame and within a certain milieu, specific kinds of music may indeed be judged harmful and undesirable, in the same way that it is commonly acknowledged that other kinds of music (especially classical as defined in its broader sense) may be beneficial to the character in arousing good or desirable feelings and thoughts in the individual. Much music has a clearly specific function in arousing predictable emotions: e.g., religious music in stirring feelings of spirituality or nearness to God, or martial music in stimulating feelings of patriotism or aggression.

To deny that music acts as a stimulant to different frames of mind is both absurd and nonsensical, and few would contradict this; but there are many in the contemporary world who are loathed to follow the consequential logic of this by admitting also that music may act as a good or bad influence. Without good reason they stop short at this point, and throw up all kinds of arguments against the idea of *proving* the harmful effects of music. This is probably because we now live in a tolerant and heterogeneous society, and we are overcome by its complexity and our own uncertainties, and we are reluctant to impute blame on anything unless the majority are also in agreement.

16 – The need to resist American power

The more widespread criticism of American youth culture, however, was not that it was corrupting in undermining good character but that it was simply time-wasting in a world which had so much more to offer. Had I been born a quarter or half a century later, I might have developed a very different personality. I am loathed to contemplate the possibility that I might then have spent my leisure hours listening to pop or in indulging an addiction to computer games. In the absence of these things I spent my free hours wandering around secondhand bookshops, seeking out literature which appealed to my senses, and later, that which I felt was self-improving.

In my early teenage years I read much of Dumas and most of the Waverley novels (something I would not repeat if I lived my life again), but in my middle and later teens, I bought and read the philosophy of Seneca, and many of the works of Cicero, and later Plato and Aristotle, and then the histories of Hume, Smollett, and Gibbon, and their contemporary, Dr. William Robertson, and these are writers who have left a lasting impression through their eternal wisdom and understanding of life and existence. No individual through his own choice, or through the help of teachers, can hope to maximise the best use of time – there is too much argumentation as to what constitutes the best to allow for that – but an honest attempt to do so is what really matters. Had I been born, therefore, a quarter of a century later, I might have fallen under the malign influence of the

American cultural onslaught which proclaims that there are no standards – or any which matter – and that the only point of life is the pursuit of a meaningless hedonism, assisted, of course, by the forgetful-inducing medium of the drugs culture.

For all these reasons, as with many millions throughout the non-American world, I fear for the future of my children and grandchildren, in facing a world where a barbarian nation is engulfing the planet with a life-style and attitudes which reverse the advancement of civilisation until it meets the level of the gutter. To stem this tide, those from the most diverse cultures must unite in friendship to meet the challenge: Arabs and Finns; Britons and Koreans; Angolans and Italians; Brazilians and Indonesians; Chinese and South Africans; Australians and Pakistanis, etc.

None of these fears existed in the world of 60 years ago when understanding and standards seemed so much clearer. There was greater clarity of thought on what constituted the good life, and greater conviction of what was bad, and seemingly, the world was ordered on greater certainties and principles. Are we therefore to say that such a world was more right or wrong in its attitudes and behaviour? Such a question we cannot answer, but we can assert that the hesitation and doubt and weakness of principle in the contemporary world, does allow for the easier penetration of the American cultural onslaught with lesser opposition. The non-American world sits passively as the great wave of the American sub-culture sweeps relentlessly across peoples and nations everywhere. The fearful tsusami is merely accepted as a fait accompli, irrespective of its damage, and most choose to meet the surge with a shrug of the shoulders and thoughtless oblivion. At least that was the situation until very recently.

But the Iraqi War and the upsurge in international terrorism may act as a catalyst, for a new consciousness is awakening in the non-American world. In the light of social discontent and widespread injustice, questions are now being asked with regard to causes and effects, and blame is being thrown back at the short-sightedness, stupidity, and tyranny of

America. The realisation is beginning to dawn that the behemoth has feet of clay, and ideas are beginning to gel in different parts of the world on the necessity of uniting to resist the foolish oppressor.

17 – Origins of the cultural-political divide between the US and non-American world

It has to be asked, what was the underlying factor or root cause which first raised the hackles of peoples worldwide against the ethos of America? It certainly had little to do with the mode of government of a people, i.e. as to whether they lived under liberal or democratic regimes, or under authoritarian dictatorships, for those in the most democratic countries as Finland, Denmark, Switzerland, or the Netherlands, have been filled with loathing and contempt for America to no lesser degree than the peoples of pre-War Spain, Germany, or Japan. The loathing is partly attributable to a natural distaste for the falseness, superficiality and hypocrisy of America, but this only goes some way towards an explanation.

The real explanation is only to be found in the fact that all peoples and cultures in the non-American world sense the need for an ideal existence whereby power relationships are expressed in terms of the most deserving, defined as both the morally good and competent. Of course the realisation of such an ideal is in practice unattainable, but the abstraction is nonetheless upheld as a constant source of hope and possibility. All societies and tribes, howsoever their mode of governance strive to ensure their leaders are perceived as the best, and when fallibility is recognised, then an aura is created through the cloak of magic, or priestly power, or divine right, or the party ideology of a democratic system.

Meanwhile, the least deserving in the community are not necessarily perceived as the morally least worthy but rather as the least competent or less fortunate. The realism of all non-American peoples, therefore, recognises the inevitability of a pecking order, and hence the existence of an aristocratic ethos underpinning the business of life. This does not necessarily entail a belief in aristocracy as a mode of government, but only recognition of the inequality and difference of all, and the need for artificial mechanisms to ensure justice and equity in society. This universal recognition of the inequality and/or difference between all underlines an honest acceptance that only the intervention of the state is capable of ensuring justice and equity within society.

Now the cultural-political ethos which arose uniquely in the pioneering spirit of American society was the very antithesis of this. The individual was falsely seen as equal and identical with every other individual, not within the idea of a structured community but within an atomised mass of people, each of whom was crazily aspiring to reach the apex of society. This theoretical view of social placement and aspirations was wholly unrealistic, but it was essential to the abstraction of American democracy. The illusion was maintained or expressed in concrete form through an exchange of easy familiarity between the different ranks of society: e.g., first name terms or informal gestures, and the constant reiteration that all were endowed with the infinite capacity to reach the top. Such a superficial style of life was riven with hypocrisy and deceit, giving rise to life promises which could never be fulfilled. But it was a deceit and hypocrisy accepted by all as a half-accepted truth, since it lay at the crux of the democratic ideology.

It arose historically through the repudiation of all systems of privilege and the ordering of ranks in the Old world, but the flight from injustice led to the invented illusions and impracticable ideals of the New world. In the first centuries of America's existence there was little need to think about the nature of a structured state or society. In the great open spaces only the individual mattered, and beyond hewing a few trees into a log cabin, and shooting game, little more was needed to satisfy mind or body. It was during these years that the American ethos was fully formed – or at least, brought to the consciousness that we know it today. But the pioneering spirit, as we have said, is unsuited and impracticable when transferred to the very different needs of the 21st century. It defies every reality when striving for a fair, democratic, egalitarian, or environmentally friendly society.

As America became a great power it was nonetheless necessary to develop a distinctive national spirit out of this morass of disparate individuals. And the irony is that through a combination of spontaneous evolution and the writings of her more significant thinkers, this supposedly "free" country developed one of the most conformist national characters in the industrialised world. The conformist attitude was not only influenced by the emptiness of her intellectual life; the lack of any tradition to draw upon the past; the constant reiteration of slogans the meanings of which were ill-defined; but by the need to repress or pass over certain factors in her history constituting an embarrassment to any country claiming democratic credentials.

18 – Hypocrisy of American Freedom and Democracy

It has to be borne in mind that for almost the first hundred years after her successful War of Independence, America was the only country of any significance in the Western world employing an institutionalised system of slavery – and a system enforced through the utmost barbarism and cruelty in both preventing escape and ensuring effective breeding methods in satisfying the demands for heavy labour. It was a system of slavery which would have shocked our ancestors of the Dark ages, and even the peoples of the ancient world where the manumission of slaves became a common practice.

It should additionally be borne in mind that one of the most vocal and voluminous apologists amongst the founders of the new Republic, for this freshly invented "freedom" and "democracy," was himself a major slave owner, and so was deeply compromised by the economic system from its beginning.[20] Are we therefore to conclude that hypocrisy was woven into the very concept of freedom and democracy from

---

[20] I.e. Thomas Jefferson.

the first day of the Republic's existence? If not, we are bound, nonetheless, to conclude that freedom was founded in collusion with the principles of slavery, together with all the injustice, oppression, suffering, and humiliation it entailed.

Although slavery was only institutionalised in the southern states, its economic repercussions were experienced on a national scale, for there was a hunger for cotton by the northern factories. In such a society, the slogans of "freedom" and "democracy" could only have been used in a kind of mindless hypocrisy, with little thought of their true meaning, and none for the concept of a universal humanity.

There is a commonly held assumption that the northern States of mid-19th century America were anti-slavery whilst the southern States were pro, but the situation was more complex than that, and the repercussions of that complexity remain until the present day. For example, whilst the Reconstruction Act of 1867 ensured the vote to black men throughout the southern States, much of the north rejected it. At the end of the Civil War only five New England States enfranchised black men, including New York on the condition they owned property, and between 1867-1869 nine referenda in northern States defeated proposals for black suffrage. The extension of the suffrage to the American Negro population was not achieved through the white conscience in fighting for justice or greater equality, but rather through expediency in consolidating the *political power* of the north over the defeated south, and this explains north-south resentment amongst the white population existing until the present day.

Whenever an ideal in society is contradicted by the facts of reality it has to be hammered home all the harder, and this is exactly what occurred in America. The truth was so unpalatable that its denial became the duty of every good American. America therefore re-invented itself as the *most free* and *most democratic* country on earth, and loudly proclaimed this from the rooftops of the world; whilst at the same time decrying all other countries as in *some way* deficient in the genuine democratic spirit. The awful realisation is that so many peoples have actually fallen for this propaganda, although they have never understood exactly how their own systems were supposedly amiss by comparison.

The natural tendency of America towards a self-enforced conformism arose psychologically as a form of retreat from the realisation of the horrors confronting society: e.g., that slavery contradicted freedom; that extreme wealth contradicted widespread poverty; that the opportunity of the few contradicted the misfortune of the many; and that power contradicted powerlessness, etc. As wealth and change were moving at too great a pace in this vast country to be comprehended by either the state or the majority, it was necessary to formulate an ideal, as a bonding mechanism, appealing to rich and poor alike.

The ideal which emerged was that of the populist culture – a phenomenon unique to America. Through its superficiality it had the virtue of inducing a useful forgetfulness of all that was inconvenient in American civilisation. Cultures normally emerge through a process of gradual evolution, but because of America's break with the past (a conscious choice) she was obliged to manufacture a synthetic culture. In ensuring its universal comprehension within the melting pot of American life, it needed to subordinate the idea of quality to that of a debasing populism designed specifically for the lowest common denominator. And an unspoken law ensured that standards were kept at a low level through the frightening threat of elitism and contravening the democratic ethos.

A populist culture was therefore maintained not through the criteria of art or aesthetics, but predominantly through fulfilling marketing needs. Creativity, therefore, did not emerge through art but through following various formulae, sometimes dictated (e.g. in the case of the film) through the collective of a management team. The marketing approach to culture killed art and spontaneity in their tracks, replacing them with self-conscious crude stereotypical invention, designed to elicit the right emotional response from the dullest imagination. Such an approach blunted subtlety of expression in remaining comprehensible to the most childlike mentality.

This is the awful reality of American culture as perceived throughout the non-American world. It penetrates every aspect of life in dragging down standards to the lowest common denominator. It begins with the Hollywood film, which through policies decided in 2005, is now degenerating into pornography and gratuitous violence merely to remain in profitability; to the dreadful cartoon banalities of Disney and their corruption of the very young throughout the globe; to the degeneration of unhealthy eating habits promoted by such multinationals as Macdonalds and KFC; and to the pop culture and its offshoots.

19 – Populism and the debasement of standards

The worst aspects of this populism stems from the fact that it kills the inclination and capacity for intelligent thought or problem-solving by the majority. In a country where all are perceived as being as good as one another; where one person's opinion is regarded as no more valid than another's; where there exists no concept of a hierarchy of knowledge or values; and where all are bidden to be dumbed-down in respecting the equality of the least clever, there is little scope for the emergence of intelligent comment or well-informed opinion. In such an environment there is no point, even, in attempting to discuss issues beyond their most superficial consideration, since there will be no listeners to meet the intellectual challenge.

This in turn represses the educational level of the majority, and such a situation is exploited by the political establishment and the power of the financial-industrial elite. One of the most perceptive of American thinkers, some one and a half centuries ago, penned with passion that he, "hated this shallow Americanism which hopes to get rich by credit, to get knowledge by raps on midnight tables, to learn the economy of the mind my phrenology, or skill without study, or mastery without apprenticeship."[21]

In such a society where the majority insist on repressing standards and values in homage to the egalitarianism of the

---

[21] R.W. Emerson, *Society & Solitude: Success.*

below average individual, even the academic elites who enter the public stage of political life are adversely influenced. This is manifested through the choice of the glamorous populist mediocre as elected representatives in preference to the scholarly and proficient. It is only the false underlying values of society which allow such a situation to exist. In those societies based on the core values of education as the criterion or measure of the good or most desirable qualities to be found in the individual, such as the Scandinavian states or the Confucian countries of China, Korea, or Japan, or the other Far East Tigers, those who wield power may be perceived as dull or elderly, but they are nonetheless highly educated and their countries are usually ruled with wisdom in maximising the prosperity of their majorities.

Such peoples as the Swedes or Singaporeans do not debase themselves in looking for film star qualities in their leaders, for they prefer the reliant and proficient in ensuring good government in serving the interests of their majorities. This contrasts sharply with the situation in America where glamour has become of such paramount importance that the politician with below average looks or height stands no chance of election. Americans do not look for brains in their politicians, for the majority are incapable of discerning intelligence if they saw it. Consequently, whilst America is the wealthiest country on earth on account of its size and industrialisation, but not (it should be noted) according to its per capita earnings and living standards, it is also amongst the worst governed of industrialised countries.

In clarifying the above in more concrete terms, examples should be cited. Not all multinationals purveying consumer goods should be exposed to criticism – but certainly those of America. For example, whilst Macdonalds, Burger King, Little Chef, KFC, Garfunkel's and Starbucks, and other American-style retail outlets instinctively arouse the ire of the thinking public on so many counts, this is not extended to such catering enterprises as Café Rouge or Chez Gerrard, or Caffé Uno, Dino's or Bella Italia. This is because the latter are not only protected by the aura of their French or Italian associations, but because of the better quality and variety of their food.

Passing to another industry: although IKEA may have a reputation for producing inexpensive furniture, and despite the many quips on the alleged difficulties of assembling their products, the design and quality of their goods are so well-established, that no one would suggest they fail to fill a genuine *social* as well as a marketing need. In addition, Sweden is a symbol of freedom and democracy worldwide, and peoples everywhere are pleased to flock to their stores and buy their products which seem to fulfil the needs of the ideal home whilst also being attainable to those on the most modest budgets. IKEA not only proudly flies a line of Swedish flags aloft a row of masts, but offers Swedish cuisine in her restaurants, and even names her merchandise in her native tongue, and all these factors seem to add credence to her business integrity. Imagine if an American outlet was to adopt a similar policy in exploiting national appeal: it would at once arouse suspicion and ridicule, whilst the sight of her flag would engender anger and contempt in the hearts of many! This is because contemporary America cannot escape the association of her status as an aggressor and oppressive power.

Besides the above factors, it has to be borne in mind that France, Italy, or Sweden do not threaten to engulf the world, either economically or culturally, and so their transnational enterprises do not arouse the fear which is always encountered when meeting the American corporation. American business is overtly and unashamedly intent on dominating the world – and proud of it to boot – in the mistaken belief that the world is so masochistically inclined as to welcome such financial domination. Such maniacal ambitions, meanwhile, are not shared by the more sober peoples of France, Italy, or Sweden.

20 – Cultural cleft between the US and non-American mindset

The failure of American business to maintain sufficient *standards of objective value* in so many marketing spheres stems primarily from the cultural attitude that investors' interests should override those of the consumer, or that pure money profits should override those of social need or the natural needs of utility. There are no other reasons which sufficiently explain the shoddiness of American life, for in ordinary circumstances, i.e. elsewhere in the world, it would be anticipated that the most powerful or wealthiest country would produce also the best products and services within a free market system. It could be suggested that Americans are innately primitive or averse to quality through the deficiency of their culture, but such an argument fails to explain entirely the failure of the free market to evolve progressively.

The same explanation may also be offered with regard to shoddiness in the world of artistic creation. A typical example might be that of the showman, Liberace, who could not have emerged as a phenomenon in any other country of the world except America. During the 1950s and 60s this fraudulent monstrosity with his permed hair, sequined waistcoats and candelabra, was fêted by the American media as the greatest pianist of all time. He gained immense wealth as an artiste, toured the world, and had his own weekly TV programme which was broadcast in many countries. What differentiated his appeal between the American and non-American audience is that whilst in the first he was regarded as a serious artiste, in the latter (amongst all sectors of society) he was regarded as a buffoon, whose attractiveness was only to be found in the degree of his freakishness.

Whilst his sentimental asides and references to "life with mother," between one piano piece and another, were received as endearing characteristics by his American audience; in the rest of the world they were received as the outrageous antics of a man who exceeded the bounds of normality. During the early

50s, whilst serving in the Army, I remember some dozens of us sitting in the packed TV hut, hooting with laughter and shouting obscenities at the sight of the American ingratiating himself with his audience with his sickly smile and gossipy anecdotes of his private life. A year or two later I was taken by my father to the Haringey Hippodrome, to sneer at this freak in the flesh having seen him so frequently on our TV screens, and I remember as we stood by the stage door afterwards, grinning with mockery, seeing a small crowd of smartly dressed women of uncertain age standing around with glazed expressions as they awaited their idol.

It may well be asked, if the world found the phenomenon of Liberace so objectionable and absurd, then why did it pack the concert halls week after week, and why did it insist, for so long, in watching the TV shows in which he starred? An answer must be given to this question, and it is to be found in the fact that he was purely a product of US marketing techniques and populism, and in the cultural field, these latter cannot be related to the objective criteria of aesthetics or quality. He was popular, not because of the way he played Chopin or Beethoven, but because of his outrageous behaviour, gestures, and style of dress, which left his audience gasping in disbelief.

The British press had no reservations in slating this fraudulent showman for his pretentiousness in presenting the classics, and eventually, Cassandra of the *Daily Mirror* went a step too far when he wrote a notorious article and poem leading to a libel case and damages for the aggrieved party. I cite these stories not to criticise any aspect of American culture or thought patterns, but only to point out the huge cleft dividing the American from the non-American mindset. In the industrialised world such a cultural division, in type or degree, is not to be found amongst any other nation or people.

21 – Money is the criterion for American value

The above does not complete the explanation of the American cultural mindset. We have covered the sociohistorical circumstances for the emergence of the pioneering spirit, and the egalitarian individual within an atomised society, and the adverse consequences of these in blocking the development of a social consciousness or the role of the state in attending to the needs of the less fortunate. But we have not yet identified the core value system of America. In the non-American world core values stem from the traditions of a people, and the system of its authority, especially as mediated objectively through religion and aesthetics.

In contemporary industrialised societies, the idea of education and knowledge in contributing to the progress and good of humanity, is increasingly accepted as the core value of peoples. In America, on the contrary, because of proletarianising democratic values, education carries little status since it is assumed to be elitist in the eyes of the majority. Hence educated or clever people are labelled "egg-heads," and remain suspect as possessing anti-social characteristics. In response to this majority ethos the educated and clever, as a defensive mechanism, feign a superficiality they do not ordinarily possess. The author, Tariq Ali, has written about the "increasingly parochial culture" (of America) "that celebrates the virtues of ignorance" and "promotes a cult of stupidity."[22]

What core cultural value was left, therefore, for the American people to embrace? The underlying value of America is the worship of money, and this is uniquely expressed through the necessity that the prime meaning or value of any object, idea or abstraction is only to be discovered through its monetary value. This is a supremely democratic idea *if the concept of democracy demands* the levelling of all humanity to an easily comprehensible understanding of life and existence. This is explained by the fact that whilst the concept of monetary value is always egalitarian, all other values are essentially hierarchical in that they exist within a spectrum of measure subject to objective criteria. Money values, on the other hand, are abstract and arbitrary, and subject to whim and subjective market forces. They can say nothing which is reliable or intelligent about the

---

[22] Tariq Ali, *The Clash of Fundamantalisms*, Verso, 202, p. 1.

measure of good or bad in the intrinsic quality of a thing, and for this reason the banalities of monetary value are easily comprehensible – even to the moron.

This is the simple and *only* explanation for the bad taste of Americans in their choice of all things, and for their philistinism and the ridicule in which they are held by the rest of the world. Through a combination of lack of cultural roots or tradition, or objective criteria for judgement, they are forced to lean on the secure foundations of monetary value in reaching their likes and dislikes. None need be ashamed in acknowledging the monetary value of a thing, for it enforces an equality of outlook, and this is particularly convenient in the spheres of art and culture. There is so much in America which non-Americans would have been ashamed to produce, but those of the former lack those natural inhibitions safeguarding good taste and the reputation of the past to be built upon, which are common qualities intrinsic to all other peoples.

22 – Monetary worth directs the American moral sense

The concept of the value of money has even penetrated deep into the American moral psyche. The man or woman who is poor, or is otherwise disadvantaged in society, is judged by the Christian and other American churches to be the victim of God's punishment for sins known or unknown, or passed down through forefathers long forgotten. American Christianity is based predominantly on the Calvinistic theories of predestination which proclaim that the fate, or goodness or badness of a person, is destined in the womb, and that this is the explanation for "sins unknown." Under this terrible belief, nothing can change God's unalterable will with regard to the outcome of human life, and many scholars from the time of Max Weber, have written about the psychological implications of the so-called Protestant work ethic.

The impoverished and those who suffer misfortune in America are overcome with shame and so retreat into isolation and fade into social insignificance. The poor have always been many or proportionally large in America, but because they have never asserted themselves as a political constituency, they have always remained pariahs hidden from the activity of the nation's life. That is, there are no significant political forces which help to readjust the economic imbalance between the different sectors of society, and this is a major fault in the American democratic system by comparison with all other democracies.

Such a mindset and such political passivity in the face of social injustice is only made possible through the concept that money is the value through which all things should be judged. The American Christian preacher, therefore, especially if he is of fundamentalist persuasion, and evangelical or Baptist, will openly declare that the rich are the blessed and deserving, whilst the poor are the undeserving who are destined by necessity to suffer the consequences of their condition. He may assent to the principles of charity but not to serious political measures in readjusting the organisation of society.

Hence the question of justice or injustice simply does not arise, and so the unfortunate must learn to live with their condition. In such an environment, in contrast with all other societies on the planet, it is impossible for political ideas to develop for changing structures to create social justice or greater egalitarianism. This explains Michael Harrington's bewailing that, "the other America, the America of poverty, is hidden today in a way that it never was before. Its millions are socially invisible to the rest of us. ... The very development of American society is creating a new kind of blindness about poverty. The poor are increasingly slipping out of the very experience and consciousness of the nation."[23]

All this returns us to the American democratic imperative for the debasement of standards, which slots in so nicely with the concept of money as the basis for value, as well as with the psychological mechanism of the Protestant work ethic. The cultural dumbing-down of the majority creates a society which is superficial, unquestioning, stupid, and easily manipulated. The powerful and influential which in America means only

---

[23] Michael Harrington, *The Other America: Poverty In The United States*, 1962, ch. 1.

those with financial power (for there are no other traditions or movements emerging from the base of society to challenge the brute force of the dollar) are able to exert total power over the nation.

Because America offers the pretence of Democracy, this power is subtle in employing the cleverest psychological tactics of advertising and propaganda, as well as all the tricks of Behaviourist philosophy (or Taylorism) in maintaining a contented or happy people. Providing the pigs are well fed and well bedded down on straw, it does not matter how soon they are led to the slaughter in serving the rentier interests of their all-powerful masters.

***

CHAPTER 4

AMERICA AND THE DEBASEMENT OF DEMOCRATIC VALUES

"The mythical America ... - that marvellous, heroic, sentimental land – was an object of faith. It challenged you to make the believer's leap over the rude facts at your feet."

Jonathan Raban, *Hunting Mr. Heartbreak*, Ch. 2, 1990.

1 – Limitations of the American concept of Freedom

Having considered the debasement of American cultural values, we must now turn to the logical consequences of this, viz., the debasement of American democratic and political values.

The terms Freedom and Democracy have a meaning which seemingly is easily understood by the majority. To the man or woman on the proverbial Clapham omnibus their definition may be obvious, but it needs to be pointed out that a facile understanding of these concepts is of little use or guidance within the context of political discussion. Every person may know what freedom means to him or her, but even such a concept may be false when digging for a deeper reality. To be free of hunger, or want of shelter, or ill health, or lack of warmth or decent clothing, etc., are obvious wants to every child and adult. There are easy answers to freedom *from* but when we turn to freedom *for*, we pose questions demanding a deeper examination.

The American understanding of freedom and democracy as elaborated through their historical tradition and popularised for majority consumption, is essentially simplistic and naïve. This is primarily because these concepts were formulated during the early modern period and prior to the complexities of an industrial civilisation. The core of their idea of freedom is taken from the philosophy of John Locke – most notably from his *Two Treatises of Civil Government*. These seminal works appeared towards the end of the 17th century, after an era of rebellion and during the first intimations of democratic government. Locke's *Treatises* present a social contract theory embodying a defence of natural rights and a justification for constitutional law, the liberty of the individual and the rule of the majority, but their main thrust in influencing American thought was the emphasis laid on the sanctity of private property.

The development of these ideas a hundred years later in the post-Independence period, assumed a society of constant growth within a pioneering environment. It was assumed that society constituted a population of free and equal property owners, the political interests of whom were enabled by a relatively non-interventionist government. The philosophy of *laissez-faire* (or letting things be) was taken from the more recently published work of Adam smith on *The Wealth of Nations*, but just as the ideas of Locke were seized upon in a superficial and piecemeal fashion, so too were those of the moral philosopher who followed a century later. American political philosophy was intensely individualistic, and the Thatcherite phrase, "there is no society only individuals," might neatly summarise its general attitude.

In such a political environment there was little consideration for alleviating the needs of the downtrodden or oppressed – and indeed, there was no recognition even of the existence of a slave population. With the advent of intensive industrialisation in the middle of the 19th century and the subsequent formation of powerful corporations, opinion-formers strengthened the myth of the infinite capacity of each and every citizen to reach the heights of wealth and power, and in this way ideas about the "reform of society" or the need for "social engineering," etc., were conveniently bye-passed. Since for so long a period in American history there was always an excess of virgin land for occupation and development – often freely available through the government for first takers – the illusion of infinite possibilities for any citizen within a country which had no need for the idea of an *organised society* has been maintained until the present day.

2 – The USA is not in origin a democracy

There is a worldwide and wholly false notion that America was established as a democracy following her War of Independence in the 1780s. This impression is confirmed by the pictorial images – of idolatrous magnitude – of the founders of the Republic signing the Constitution, of George Washington, their first President, in addition to other emotive illustrations of striking historical events, and always they are associated with the idea of Democracy emboldened in capital letters.

The truth is that a careful reading of the Declaration of Independence as signed in Congress on 4th July 1776, or The Articles of Confederation and Perpetual Union of the original thirteen States of 15th November 1777, or the Constitution of the United States of America, as signed by George Washington and thirty eight others, do not contain a single reference to the term "democracy." Authoritative sources clearly state that the Declaration of Independence "was a demand for constitutional, and *not* for democratic government, and the colonial assemblies of the period, though based on a somewhat broader franchise than the British parliament, were far from being democratic bodies."[24] Furthermore, the Constitution which emerged from the subsequent deliberations of the 1780s "was a compromise between democratic and anti-democratic ideas."[25]

One of the most prominent American historians of the first half of the last century, Charles A. Beard, demonstrated in his penetrating book, *An Economic Interpretation of the Constitution*, published in 1913, that the makers of the Constitution of 1787 had served the interests of the moneyed classes of their day. Both Jefferson and Madison had eschewed including the term "democratic" within the name of a political party as being too radical in its connotations, although the former was elected as President in 1801 on a Democratic-Republican ticket, and we can take this as the first reference to the term in American political history.

---

[24] *Encyclopaedia Britannica*, 1963, Vol. 7, p. 218.
[25] Ibid.

In view of the above facts it should therefore be no surprise that America soon mutated into a plutocratic state with scant support for the poorer sectors of her population. The idea that America was originally founded as a democracy is therefore clearly a fiction which needs to be repudiated. It is an invented myth to inspire the patriotism of her people and to give some sustenance to the downtrodden in her midst; in the same way that ancient Rome and Greece invented myths to give greater credence to their various political systems.

3 – Why Freedom is better understood in the non-American world

In these respects a sharp contrast is to be found between American history and that of the rest of the world. Although America has experienced two *political revolutions* if one includes the War of Independence (1776-1782) and the Civil War (1861-1865), she has never experienced a *social revolution* in any way approaching those of Europe in the 18th or 19th centuries, and neither has she developed a deep political consciousness of those divisions marking the economic interests of separate groups. For obvious historical reasons, i.e. the emergence of nation states from feudalism and entrenched privilege to industrialisation, all Europe and other countries further afield, experienced the tribulations of class conflict through which they evolved towards greater justice and equity.

The American might respond to this realisation with the exclamation, "and good avoidance too,!" but the lack of this social conflict, and the experience which it brings, has left him with a deficient impression of political truth. The European, on the other hand, has a very sophisticated political consciousness, and consequently, he can recognise social injustice and inegalitarianism with greater clarity than his American cousin. The European and Far East citizen, and others, are able to identify social problems and resolve them within the context of legislative reform, e.g., through the safety net of old age pensions, and benefits for sickness or unemployment.

Such benevolent inclinations are anathema to mainline American thinking, where each individual is supposedly responsible for himself, and it is only with great reluctance and during periods of extreme hardship, such as the Great Depression of the 1930s followed by the New Deal, that America has ever been prevailed upon to introduce legislation for alleviating stress. And such periods of occasional reform are not cherished in the collective memory of the majority. In retrospect, such reformers as F.D. Roosevelt are seen as having "patronised" the poor and unfortunate, or having been responsible for legislation which should never have been contemplated in the first place. Several books have recently appeared along the lines that the New Deal contradicted the ethos of American political life through promoting an "ugly collectivism" which threatened the initiative of the individual.

This is in sharp contrast to European attitudes where the memories of Bismarck of the 1880s, or Asquith and Lloyd George during the Liberal administration of 1906-1911, or Attlee and Aneurin Bevan in the post-War period, are all held in high regard because of the milestones they created in bringing about more egalitarian and just communities. The European and others realise that in the discussion of political life freedom and democracy are complex concepts, and that liberty and equality need to achieve a perfect balance in reaching the demands of a free and just society.

When the American concept of freedom is applied to the modern industrialised society, it is always fraught with the contradiction of *my* freedom versus *your* freedom, and as the individual is always pitted against the collective as contrasted with *cooperating* with the collective, it is always the powerful with *their* freedom which predominates above all other interests. When you cannot achieve *your* freedom then you are undeserving of it since you lack sufficient determination and ability. The theory is that all freedoms are equally open to all and are there for the grabbing, but this, of course, takes no account of the diversity of human abilities and the multiplicity of needs.

4 – The brutality of US industrial relations

The brutality and ruthlessness of the American authorities when confronted by labour unrest, and the repeated failure of workers to achieve their ends, is a leitmotif of American history, in sharp contrast to the European experience and the successful achievement of workers' rights. On numberless occasions American workers have been gunned down by the police. In 1877 the Pennsylvania coal miners striking in response to wage cuts were not only fired from their employment but evicted from their homes. In the same year a nationwide series of railroad strikes ignited by a wage reduction on the Baltimore and Ohio railroad, led to the newly installed President Rutherford B. Hayes, calling out the troops, resulting in the deaths of almost a hundred strikers.

Far from evoking moral indignation (as would have been the case in any part of Europe), the religious press responded hysterically, and in the words of a Congregational journal, "If the club of the policeman, knocking out the brains of the rioter, will answer, then well and good, (but if not) then bullets and bayonets ... constitute the remedy."[26] On May Day in 1886 340,000 workers struck in support of the campaign for an 8-hour day, and the city of Cincinnati was virtually shut down for almost a month. In the same year the Chicago police shot and killed four strikers at the McCormick Harvester plant on 3rd May. At a protest rally on the following day in the city's Haymarket square, a bomb was thrown from a nearby building, killing or fatally wounding seven policemen, and the latter responded by firing wildly into the crowd killing four demonstrators.

The public reaction was immediate. Most the sponsors of the protest were associated with a German language newspaper, the *Arbeiter Zeitung*, and eight were arrested and tried. The Illinois attorney general declared: "Convict these men, make examples of them. Hang them, and you save our institutions." Although no evidence connected them directly with the bomb

---

[26] Paul S. Boyer, et al, *The Enduring Vision*, 2nd ed., 1993, D.C. Heath & Co., Lexington, MA, p. 615.

throwing, all were convicted and four were executed, and one committed suicide in prison.[27] Many other examples of brutality against working people could be cited during the same period, or indeed, continuing until well into the middle of the 20th century.

One of the most notorious atrocities against strikers occurred in May 1937 when workers in 27 Little Steel plants, including Republic's grimy factory in south Chicago walked off the job. Anticipating the strike, Tom Girder, a known union hater assembled an arsenal of riot guns and tear gas. On 30th May, Memorial Day, a mass of strikers approached a force of 264 police guarding the factory, and when a large stick was thrown at the police, the latter responded with a hail of bullets which left four strikers dead, six others dying, and more than eighty wounded. Following an enquiry, a coroner's jury ruled the killings as "justifiable homicide."

It is hard to imagine that such an episode or its outcome could have occurred in any other industrialised country, except perhaps, in Soviet Russia. In America, many employers required their workers to sign "yellow dog" contracts in which they promised not to strike or join a union. Socialism as a means towards the advancement of human rights was never considered as an option by significant political or intellectual elites in America. Its worth was never even evaluated for its own merits, for it was prejudicially condemned as a "foreign," and most specifically, as a German cause, which had no relevance within the framework of American politics.

With regard to labour unrest during the last quarter of the 19th century, there is a remarkable resemblance to similar events in Russia during the same period. The American government was no less bloodthirsty in crushing the natural aspirations of working people than the Tsarist regime in the 19th and early 20th centuries. A significant difference, however, is that in Tsarist Russia, prominent personalities and aristocrats fought hard to reform institutions, but America was pitifully lacking in men or women of such foresight or social conscience.

---

[27] Ibid., p. 615.

Despite widespread injustice and poverty, the spirit of America continued along the lines of social regression. For example, Andrew Carnegie in an influential essay, *The Gospel of Wealth*, published in 1889, wrote that, "The law of competition may be sometimes hard for the individual, (but) it is best for the race, because it ensures the survival of the fittest in every department. We accept and welcome, therefore, ... the concentration of business, ... in the hands of a few; and the law of competition between these, as being not only beneficial but essential to the progress of the race."

The truth, of course, is that this falsely applied political Darwinism, has led to the worsening of the American race. Again, the cruel-minded Yale professor, William Graham Sumner, wrote in his 1883 book, *What The Social Classes Owe To Each Other*, "A drunkard in the gutter is just where he ought to be. ... The law of the survival of the fittest was not made by man, and it cannot be abrogated by man. We can only, by interfering with it, produce the survival of the unfittest." Sumner writes cynically about the "labour fakers" intent on uplifting the poor and needy, arguing that the former were actually harming the "forgotten man," i.e. the hard-working uncomplaining employee.

In such an environment, the words which Walt Whitman wrote in 1879, after observing three men rummaging through rubbish to find food, strike the ear as morally refreshing: "If the United States ... are ... to grow vast crops of poor, desperate, dissatisfied, nomadic, miserably-waged populations, such as we see looming upon us of late years ... then our republican experiment, notwithstanding all its surface-success, is at heart an unhealthy failure."

5 – When a Democracy becomes a Plutocracy

Except during brief periods of civil strife American democracy has always had a low level of ideological appeal. Although Democrats are seen as left-leaning and the Republicans are right-leaning, they cannot properly be described as left or right movements in the European sense. The situation is further complicated by the fact that the two parties represent different causes in different parts of the country. Although left and right parliamentary movements in Europe converge more closely today than they have ever done before, such convergence has always existed in America, whilst Socialism in any form has never captured the imagination of her people.   Personalities rather than ideas have acted as an inspirational force, and because of this, superficiality has suffused the entire democratic process.

In this environment elections and their mechanisms have come to be seen as the true end and purpose of democracy itself, but of course, this is very far from how the truth should be perceived. Elections become great jamborees for cheerleaders, and the celebration of crowds, but such events have little meaning and hardly express the underlying purpose of democracy. A country may hold elections whilst being far from democratic. Ancient Rome is usually cited as such an example, but much nearer our own time, we might cite the East bloc dictatorships, all of whom held regular elections. It is not suggested that American democracy should be compared with that of the Soviet bloc, for the American system is far more subtle in its managing public relations.

The constant reiteration of the word "democracy" together with all the paraphernalia of electoral processes has beguiled the American people that they actually live in a democratic society and that they are ruled by a democratic government. The reality, unfortunately, is that both these assumptions are false. America is in reality a plutocracy, i.e. ruled by the power of wealth. The criterion for a democracy is that all should enjoy the *practical* as opposed to merely the *theoretical* possibility of exerting political power, if not directly, as in Switzerland or ancient Athens, then through a representative system.

In America this is just not possible, since the financial muscle of multi-millionaires and powerful corporations have bought their way into the political system and control all the levers of power. Even the elected power of the President and his government cannot carry through electoral promises (as recently occurred with Bill Clinton's administration) when they cross the vested interests of the financial or industrial establishment. Not only are all nominations for office mediated through representatives of financial power, but government itself acts as an arm of big business in securing the power of the wealthy.

Plutocratic government may be preferable to military government, but both are unimaginative and marked by a paucity of ideas with regard to benevolent rule. The answer of America to all problems of poverty, famine, and disease in the Third World, is typical of a plutocracy, and is always the same: viz., invest or lend at a high rate of interest, so that the poor are further indebted until their oppression becomes unbearable. And this is what ordinary Americans like to describe as their charitable disposition!

6 – The non-American world has a better understanding of democracy

American democracy is bereft of underlying social purpose, or other clearly defined aim, apart from carrying out the capricious will of the isolated individual; and in this respect it differs from democracy elsewhere. In Europe and the Far East, democracy is understood as a moral and social force for the evolution of humanity to a higher sphere of existence. Elections and elected mechanisms are merely seen as the instruments towards this purpose, and not, as in America, as ends in themselves. Hence the outward trappings of democracy in the non-American world are conducted in a quieter frame of mind, with a greater concentration on ideals and substantive policies to be achieved, rather than on the glamour surrounding its candidates for office.

For the greater part of American history, the wide open spaces and the opportunity for pioneering has allowed for extreme individualism in political life. But this has given rise to few ideas on the concept of the good society, and those ideas have been presented in a thousand variations, and the inevitable outcome has been the emergence of strong convictions within a conformist and homogeneous framework. Since conventional thinking has been so seldom challenged, this has made Americans chauvinistic rather that patriotic, with their worship of the national flag, the daily solemn oath-taking of their primary schoolchildren, their love of militarism and parades,[28] and their arrogant assertion that the American political system alone should be presented as a paradigm for the future of the world.

Such characteristics are typified by Ron Kovic (played by Tom Cruise) in Oliver Stone's 1989 film, *Born On The Fourth of July*, about a super-patriot whose only desire in life is to fight for his country in Vietnam. This foolish young man, the tragic victim of a vicious educational system, is wounded and paralysed from the chest down, and returns to an America which is greatly changed from the country he left. It is a story of misguided idealism, political naivety, and national disillusion at the realisation of foreign policy failure, and all these failings are traceable to the conformism and naivety of American political life.

The countries of the non-American world, on the other hand, have always been stirred by the ferment of conflicting ideas, and this has given rise to enormous creativity and experimentation in politics. It is not always necessary that countries should experience the upheaval of revolution to realise this breadth of experience, but it is necessary that they have a long historical tradition interrupted by change and the clash of economic vested interest groups. All Europe, for example, has been divided for centuries between the conflicting interests of the Church, the feudal nobility, the peasantry, urban artisans, and wealthy merchants, and these complex divisions transcend the more simplistic class divisions as analysed by Marx and his adherents.

---

[28]   In this context it may be noted that the ideas for the mass rallies of the Nazis in arousing popular appeal were all inspired by the American political system. The man responsible for introducing Hitler to the psychological techniques of American political life was the American-German, Putzi (Ernst) Hanfstaengl, early in the 1920s. He later became head of the Foreign Press Bureau in Berlin, and when I met him in his Munich home in 1965, he confessed the significance of American campaign methods as a major factor for the triumph of Nazism. He was a one-time friend of both the Roosevelt presidents.

The divisions cannot simply be explained as one sector of society oppressing another, but more often, as a duel for pre-eminence amongst those of almost equal power. These conflicts have given rise to a huge literature of political theory from the Middle Ages until the present day, and to thousands of political groups jostling to seize the state or influence government policy. Consequently, the collective memory of this historical experience has produced a highly sophisticated and politically literate public throughout Europe and elsewhere in the world, and because of this, America is in no position whatsoever to present herself as the arbiter of political wisdom.

7 – How America repudiated the politics of justice

As the absence of left of centre movements is one of the most significantly defining political differences between America and the rest of the world, something more must be explained about the historical background of this. The radical movements which did emerge and capture the imagination of millions, comprised a strange mix of progressive and reactionary ideas, often within a religious context, and they were further complicated not by appealing to the poor and oppressed across all sectors of society, but by appealing to the needs of specific interest groups.

For example, the People's Populist party of the 1890s, led by William Jennings Bryan, was predominantly a rural movement fighting against the rentier exploitation of the farming class, which was bankrupted and impoverished by the lending of unscrupulous merchants for the purchase of agricultural machinery and the modernisation of methods. In attempting to counter the widespread dispossession of smaller farmholdings, the Populists advocated an increase in the price of agricultural products, and this in turn led to conflict with the interests of the urban proletariat led by William McKinley and the Republican party. Against such a pattern of politics it became impossible to represent the interests of the poor or economically oppressed on an all-nation basis.

The left of centre movement which timewise overlapped and then superseded Populism was the urban Progressive movement, but the Progressivists comprised a diverse range of political and intellectual activists, and they were reformers rather than radicals or revolutionaries. Whilst they were supported by a number of prominent thinkers, their political weakness lay in an exaggerated confidence in the social applications of science, e.g. eugenics. Their readiness to use state power in coercing individual behaviour was seen as repressive and even destructive, whilst their record on racial issues was dismal.

Meanwhile, a Marxist oriented Socialist Labour party had been established in 1877 by a small group of primarily German-born immigrants, but its total ineffectiveness may be measured by the fact that in 1890 it had only raised its membership to a total of 1,500. In 1900 the more successful Socialist party was formed by Russian-Jewish and German immigrants, and others, and by 1912, at the peak of their strength, they had a membership of 118,000. During the elections of 1908 they succeeded in capturing 2.8% of the popular vote, and during that of 1916 3.2%, and on the last occasion in 1920 3.4%.

Socialism, the only intellectually serious left wing ideology, was therefore rejected as an alien creed, never to gain a foothold in America, except amongst groups of recent immigrants from Continental and Eastern Europe. The structure of American politics in conjunction with the mindset of her people living on the myth of the American dream was therefore enough to ensure the non-viability of any left of centre movement. But more significant was the consequence of this failure: viz., the inability of a people to raise sufficient compassion within itself to appreciate or fight for social justice or equity.

If we turn to political legislation, we can trace the influence of the great corporations in blocking needed reform in the immediate post-War era. The Republicans of the 80th Congress, convened in January 1947, interpreted the 1946 elections as a mandate to reverse the New Deal. Senator Robert

A. Taft of Ohio (known as "Mr. Republican"), insisted that, "We have got to break with the corrupting idea that we can legislate prosperity, legislate equality, legislate opportunity." The Republican controlled Congress then quickly passed tax measures favouring the wealthy and defeated a proposal to raise the minimum wage. They then vowed to "meat-axe government frills," and rebuffed Truman's requests for Federal aid to education and a comprehensive housing programme.

The Democrat, Harry S. Truman, was one of the better Presidents of America, but in 1947 he was unable to prevent the passing of the Labour-Management Relations Act (better known as the Taft-Hartley Act) which outlawed such practices as the closed shop, and legislated for conditions on strike action; and meanwhile, more than twenty States passed a variety of laws restricting union activities. Worse still, two years later, Congress refused Truman's proposals for a comprehensive national health insurance plan, and a crop-subsidy system that would both maintain farm incomes and hold down food prices. All these were defining measures which further divided America from the enlightened reforming spirit of Europe and the Far East in the immediate post-War period.

8 – American democracy corrupted by a debasing populism

Most peoples in the non-American world have been nurtured in crowded societies offering no open spaces for pioneering development. Consequently, they have developed in a cheek by jowl environment, often alongside those with whom they had little in common or were in political or religious conflict. This led eventually to attitudes of toleration and compromise, and most notably, to a healthy scepticism and acceptance of difference of a kind which is almost unknown in America.

The European social environment is liberal and one of grey on grey, whilst in America it is a stark black or white, reflecting a conservatism and guarded suspicion of everything which fails to match the conformist pattern. For all the above reasons, therefore, and because America can no longer offer undeveloped tracts of land to her people, it is Europe and the Confucian countries of the Far East, which should be offering a political paradigm for the future of the world, and not the US. The people of the US already face the same problems as those of the rest of the world, but she has not yet awoken to the harsh fact that the pioneering spirit together with her concept of freedom and democracy is quite outdated and bankrupt in the world of the 21st century.

But the greatest impediment confronting the American people for the development of a more perceptive political consciousness stems from their particular brand of democratic populism and the cultural dumbing-down of the majority. In the previous chapter we considered the debasement of cultural values, and now we must turn to the debasement of democratic and political values.

And this brings us to the greatest conundrum implied in democracy itself. Democracy means the rule and will of the majority, but what if that majority fails to represent the best or most desirable values for society? This is a question which has never irked the American consciousness and hence her people have been unafraid in pursuing a debasing populism often seen as of the worst possible kind. The non-American world, on the other hand, has always been constrained in the pursuit of uninhibited populism through the traditions of an established culture and the need to sustain existing standards. In this respect, therefore, the non-American world may be seen as attempting to hold back those forces intrinsic to the very purpose and spirit of democracy, but we are now presenting a thesis which is the very opposite of this.

In the previous chapter we touched on the dumbing-down of high culture, and explained how the reduction of all values to monetary values contributed to a debasing populism. Here we must reiterate, once again, that no criticism is being made of any specific American art form *per se*, and that "low culture" is as valid as entertainment or enlightenment as high culture. Furthermore, attempts to make value comparisons between

Presley or Prokofiev are repudiated as nonsense, since they exist in different musical worlds and only like can be compared with like.

There are art forms which in origin are specific to America, such as jazz or the musical, and these may be enjoyed and judged according to their own particular standards. The present author admits to enjoying the American musical for its mixture of skills in dancing, singing, acrobatic feats, etc., but the musical cannot be compared with opera which exists in quite a different sphere and is judged according to other criteria. American art forms are therefore no less valid than those of Europe, Japan, India, or elsewhere, but they are *different*, and as with all art should be judged according to the quality of performance and accepted standards.

We are therefore not here concerned with any particular American art forms *per se*, but rather with the general cultural environment within which all art and life is able to flourish. That is, we are concerned with a debasing populist mindset or framework within which cultural life is obliged to exist. And within such a framework, both good and bad art will emerge – although the banal, mediocre, or worthless will inevitably tend to predominate. But in this chapter we are not concerned with cultural creativity, or as to whether it may be good, bad or indifferent, but rather with the populist mindset as it affects society in general and especially the direction of political life.

9 – The problems of populism

It is necessary to offer a critique of debasing populism, since although it may only marginally affect the educated minority, it most certainly adversely affects the mentality of the majority. Although the argument may be presented that democracy demands populist measures, howsoever they may be interpreted; the opposite argument may also be put, viz., that if democracy is to be workable as an improving social influence, it is dependent on a thoughtful, intelligent, and educated majority, and such qualities are incompatible with a debasing populism.

In the non-American world until the very recent past, another argument was forwarded for democratic populism, although it did not include, of course, the epithet "debasing." Old Socialism everywhere glorified the working class and working class values and attributes, in the war against the bourgeoisie, and they promoted populism, firstly, in advancing that which was familiar and agreeable to working class people; and secondly, in undermining the values of the middle class. Populism was therefore used by Old Socialists as a strategy in the class war in further differentiating friends from foes; but beyond that specific purpose, it remained a populism which was nonetheless debasing.

Although it may have contributed to the solidarity of collectivism, it did nothing to raise the individual to a higher level in the community, or to enable the individual to otherwise better his chances culturally, educationally, or careerwise. The cultural populism of Old Socialism took such forms as the working class flat cap, pride in dirty fingernails, and particular modes of speaking, all of which helped to enhance class consciousness but did nothing to improve the lot of those intent on exerting their individuality and finding their way in the world. It was a populism which imprisoned the poor and under-privileged within the narrow confines of their origins.

The populism of the non-American world is therefore distinctive from that of America which was and is motivated by a gesture to extend the common touch to all and sundry, and to instil the deception that all are equal in the New world "democracy." The populist egalitarianism of America was only made credible to her majority through a combination of individualism within a non-interventionist state in a pioneering environment. It could never have been made acceptable within a sophisticated political society fraught with political conflict amongst many functional groups; and clearly it could never have been made acceptable in any society with a tradition of hierarchies. The absurdity of such a situation would always have broken through the actuality of hypocrisy.

The debasing cultural and political populism of America is a huge handicap to the social development of her people, for until it is finally overcome, there is little chance for achieving political maturity. It acts as a mental block to the emergence of a higher consciousness, and the awareness of all to the social ills which are hidden from the majority. America lingers in the darkness of a false consciousness, and most significantly, she cannot hope to achieve the status of a free and democratic society until such time as she has educated herself in the true ways of the world.

Although the cultural populism of Old Socialism in the non-American world is on the surface more degrading and humiliating than that of the American category, since it overtly prevents the individual from self-improvement or "rising above his station," both are equally malign in maintaining socio-political disempowerment. Whilst the cultural populism of Old Socialism enforced a uniformity and collectivism leading inevitably to an external dictatorship from above, usually referred to as the dictatorship of the proletariat; the cultural populism of America led to the glib ideology and conviction that all were equally endowed with infinite capacity, and under the smokescreen of this, the financially powerful were able to manipulate and control the majority with impunity. Whilst the Socialist society was more brutal in its exertion of power; the populist outcome of American plutocracy is more subtle and covert, although nonetheless unscrupulous in its purpose.

10 – Comparison between Superficial and Real freedom

This returns us to considering the realities of freedom and democracy. The great fallacy of the American understanding of freedom is that its concept relies on the philosophical empiricism of 17th and 18th century thinkers. That is, its definition is based on *sense perception*, which is sound in so far as it identifies *partial freedom* arising from immediate wants, but full freedom through the greater development of individual potential transcends such a restricted methodology.

For example, there are circumstances when the outcome of sense perception may be deceptive or even harmful to individual interests if cognition or consequent actions are not the outcome of a higher consciousness. Not only is sense perception *not* necessarily the best guide to decision-making or wisdom, but moreover, it is not the criterion on which reality or the nature of existence can be accurately based. Hence, in understanding *full freedom*, it is necessary to turn to the Idealists who critically examined and transcended the empiricists in depth of understanding in their definitive work from the end of the 18th and throughout the 19th centuries.

In America it is commonly assumed that freedom means nothing more nor less than the right to free choice, but in the complex world of human society and psychological motives, this would amount to a deficient understanding of freedom. Of course, in the historical past, it was always the powerful who made choices for the majority on the grounds that they knew better – irrespective of whether this concerned the way people thought, or the way they acted. Hence the banner of freedom was raised against such authority in insisting on the right to choice, and there is suspicion of anything which hinders this right. But there are clearly circumstances when free choice can lead to misfortune or regrets when its outcome leads to the *loss of freedom*. Hence there are circumstances when free choice leads to loss of freedom rather than its gain.

Clearly we do not and *could not* allow small children the right to absolute free choice. We rather guide and direct them, and expose them to selections from which they are invited to make free choice. The culture of a society operates within a framework of rules and customs allowing for free interaction and communication amongst all, and these rules and customs need to be learned and taken aboard if the individual is to benefit fully from what society has to offer.

But even within the framework and constraints of society, individuals differ vastly from one another, and even amongst closely-knit and seemingly homogeneous groups, each will in some way influence the others adversely in ways which are unknown and may never be uncovered. This is because each individual has intrinsic characteristics and potential which are not only unknown to his peers but often to himself. Within any group, dominant personalities, often unintentionally, set standards or examples with regard to thinking, taste, moral judgements, leisure pursuits, etc., and these give rise to a false consciousness in others, not so much in matters of general opinion but in matters of action and direction as adopted by specific individuals.

The most striking example of such an outcome – and it is all-important to the future of an individual – is career choice. Many, if not most, decide on their future according to the influences of peer pressure rather than according to their own intrinsic abilities and psychological temperament. They do this, not because they want to follow in the wake of their friends, or retain the friendships of youth, but because they usually do not and cannot know their own best career potential. It is often not until many years have passed, with hindsight and maturity, that the nasty realisation dawns that a life has been wasted in an occupation for which one has an indifferent capacity or quite the wrong temperament.

Hence the above cites an example of when free choice may be made during a crucial period of life, and the decision is unfortunate, and the outcome was a spoilt life and ruined potential. Not only is such an outcome a misfortune for the individual, but take any nation state and multiply this situation by several million times, and you uncover an economic and social tragedy on a major scale. What is the answer to such a catastrophe? It is not to remove free choice, but to re-define it and re-create it as a greater reality.

The free individual is not the person intent on maximising free choice, for that only leads to hedonism or meaningless acquisitiveness, but the person intent on maximising his potential as an all-rounded human being, intellectually, spiritually, and physically. These are the practical reasons why we must turn to the Idealist philosophers, rather than the

Empiricists, for a profounder understanding of the meaning of freedom.

11 – Necessary conditions for the achievement of full freedom

The American cultural ethos and concept of freedom, on the other hand, is merely primitive, for it drives the individual towards the unattainable goal of constant acquisition, usually through the perversion of the Protestant work ethic.

The answer to the misguided careerwise individual, then, is not the assertion of *blind* free choice, but rather the right to institutionalised professional guidance early in life. All pre-school leavers should be offered extensive psychological testing in conjunction with an advisory service to a cross-section of occupations. At that point in life equality of opportunity should be maximised in benefiting both the individual and the state, and although many will pass on to university, the purpose of a career service should be to clarify desires rationally, and to direct young people onto vocational rather than onto unfocused general academic courses. The outcome of such a strategy would see the implementation of true freedom.

To achieve freedom, therefore, it is necessary for a person to know Himself or Herself, but it needs the skills and expertise of a good educational system, as well as other agencies, to bring this into fruition. Free choice only then becomes meaningful decision-making.

But much more is required than the organisation for meaningful free choice in maximising the freedom of the individual. As the Greeks argued, there has to be a nicely developed balance between the intellectual, spiritual, and physical faculties in enabling wisdom of choice, for without this there may arise discontent or hurt or depression or tendencies to anti-social behaviour. An unbalanced or disturbed personality cannot enjoy full freedom. As soon as the healthy individual is free of essential wants, he then turns to the question of freedom for fulfilment, and this entails the need for a meaningful existence within society, usually expressed through work, or public service, or the nurture of children for their own sake and the benefit of the community.

The freedom which accompanies a meaningful existence within society is only attained through cultural integration, for there has to be that essential understanding and easy communication, which in turn assists towards successful participation in the democratic activities of the community. It is only then when people enjoy a rational control over their own lives, and as Hegel has argued convincingly, that political freedom is properly experienced.

As soon as a meaningful existence is achieved, the discerning individual turns towards acquiring a greater understanding of the world and humanity, and this is learned through the enjoyment of the arts and the on-going acquirement of general knowledge and experience. All this contributes to the greater freedom of the individual, since it widens choice, extends the understanding of what matters most, and puts down pointers with regard to inclinations and personal ability.

But the hope for such freedom can never be experienced by the majority in a country such as America dominated by a debasing populism which sets a ceiling on cultural life. In a country dominated by the proliferation of what is most saleable, and by the ephemeral and worthless, there is little opportunity for the masses to understand the nature of existence – let alone themselves. In a media-frenzied world of Disney cartoons, three-minute News summaries, intensive advertising, time-wasting game shows, and Jumbo burgers, there is little chance for even the thoughtful to break away from the hellish noise and images of the trivial and superfluous. In such a society humanity itself is degraded by the sight of the naked dollar stripping and dancing to enhance its own enrichment.

12 – Establishing electoral mechanisms not sufficient to create a democracy

In turning from the issue of Freedom to that of Democracy an even grimmer picture emerges. Democracy as a form of government is only workable if its subjects reach a sufficient educational level.

Furthermore, a democracy is only workable if its people are thoughtful and pro-active in contributing ideas to the good of the whole. Any nation state can establish the formal mechanisms for democratic government, but that does not create a democracy. So-called democracies have been established throughout the neo-colonial world, and although the outward forms of electoral processes may have been retained, most have soon lapsed into dictatorships of the worst possible kind, and their peoples have sunk into a morass of poverty, disease and famine.

Throughout most of Africa, for example, a sense of nationality amongst the majority has never been allowed to develop, partly because of arbitrary frontiers dividing tribal territories, and partly because tribal loyalties transcended all others in matters of political organisation. But those factors apart, the successful implementation of democracy either requires that a country has already reached a high level of civilisation and understanding, as with Japan, Korea or China, or else has already developed its democracy after a long historical process, as with Britain, Switzerland or France.

It is impractical to impose adopted models of European representative systems on purely tribal societies as has been attempted in Africa and elsewhere. How, then, can democracy be brought to these poor and oppressed peoples? Only by first identifying the true purpose and function of democracy as *people power*, and then introducing direct (as contrasted with representative) systems into ever broader functional spheres of life. Democracy, therefore, must be founded at the grass roots where ordinary people are exposed to its direct experience, in conjunction with ethical teaching on rights, obligations, liberty and equality. In this way, and through the gradual adaptation of local customs, distinctive but real modes of democracy will emerge and penetrate upwards until eventually absorbing all sectors of the nation state.

So many experiments of the past 60 years were doomed to failure because trust was placed in the elitist principle of educating cadres picked from privileged tribal members, before returning them to oversee the foundation of democracies on the European model. No account was taken of the traditional mindset of this newly educated minority, or the impossibility of their hoping to transform the thinking of majorities to accept institutions or modes of practice so alien to their own experience. Faced by an impossible task, these new leaders can hardly be blamed, therefore, if they were pushed by inevitable circumstances into presiding over states which mutated into dictatorships due to the paucity of education amongst the majority in meeting the demands of modernity. These are the reasons why in developing territories effective, true, or long-lasting democracy can only be introduced at the base of society and not imposed from its apex.

The tragedy of Africa, and other territories of the world, is that the failure of the well-meant intentions of the European powers has left an anarchic legacy which is now exploited by the ruthlessness of American capital in compounding all the problems of the past. Hence in the near future it will fall to the benevolence and moral responsibility of these European powers to confront America with its ill-intentions, and then establish advisory bodies and internal investing institutions (as described in Section 14 in Chapter 1 of this book) to ensure the foundation of sound democracies.

13 – The American System is corrupted by high finance

Leaving aside the situation of democracy in the developing world, we must return to the more relevant issue of its failure in America. If the peoples of the developing world have not yet attained a sufficient awareness or educational level for democratic government this is no reflection on their underlying character, but it *is so* in the case of the American majority. This is because America is an advanced industrial state with all the educational networks in place to facilitate the existence of a true democracy.

On paper America is a perfect democracy (and so was the Soviet Union if judged by its Constitution) and it is blessed by all manner of checks and counter-balances, and open tribunals for the inspection of candidates standing for office. The eminent British jurist and statesman, James Bryce, in his classic, *The American Commonwealth*, published in 1888, concluded that the American system of democracy could hardly be improved upon. And yet today, not only does American democracy fail miserably on every count, but it can no longer be correctly given the appellation "democratic." As we have said, the country is instead a plutocracy.

American democracy has been corrupted totally by the power of money, and it is only thanks to a system of universal hypocrisy (or the compliment which virtue pays to vice) that Americans can still spout the word "democracy" and yet keep a straight face. On the surface, American democracy may still be open and subject to checks and balances, but as offices are bought or sold by big business, or their candidates sponsored by the same, this in no way diminishes the degree of corruption.

As their glamorous politicians deliver solemn promises and morally uplifting speeches to the hysterical applause of credulous crowds, the former have no intention of keeping faith with their followers or even connecting with their needs. This is because American politicians are no more than highly paid automatons of one corporation or another, who write their speeches and direct their thought patterns. Whilst the American politician nominally represents the electorate, in reality he represents the interests of high finance, and so in duty to his sponsors, his sole responsibility is to maximise votes by any means available.

But the corruption of political life is not necessarily the ultimate criterion in the critique of a political system, although it remains so in the case of America. For example, there are many poor countries which are corrupt due to the poverty of the middle class and those in government office. During a long business career I have on occasion needed to authorise bribes to officials who could not be expected to survive on their measly government salaries, and so a culture of baksheesh has developed to enable the completion of contracts, and this is a situation which is recognised as an unfortunate necessity throughout the business world. But such a culture of corruption cannot be compared with the worse situation which exists in America, where it is driven by the greed of the powerful and wealthy in maximising their profits, and not by the poor striving to make ends meets.

14 – The de-humanisation of life

The ultimate critique of American democracy, therefore, should be judged by its final outcome for good or ill. It should not be judged so much according to its corruption, or the degree of its deception, but according to the fact that it has given rise to such a vulnerable, vicious, and rotten society; and the success or failure of any society must be assessed by the characteristics of its majority. Here we have the wealthiest nation on earth, with huge natural resources, and still with wide open spaces, and all the potential for creating the best and happiest people on the planet.

Instead we find a nation polarised between rich and poor, with no effective safety net for the latter in terms of sickness or unemployment benefit, or old age pensions; a gun culture with the highest criminality rate in the world; a prison population which exceeds per capital that of any other country; and a frenetic population working longer hours and with shorter holidays than those of any other advanced industrial economy.

A closer look at the US economy reveals that some three quarters of American wage earners saw their average wage decline from $331 per week in 1973 to $280 in 2003, allowing for inflation. The growth of the economy during this period went to the tiny elite of the rich and powerful: in 1960 this group was paid 41 times the average production wage of American workers, but by 2005 this figure is roughly 300 times the US average production wage.

Income inequality in America is now approaching Third world levels. When wages in a Rentier economy fall behind productivity, as has occurred in the US since the mid-70s, then profits will rise as a percentage of GDP. This enhanced Rentier profitability in turn will lead to a rise in share values resulting in a bull market for equities. And this is the familiar scenario of the boom-bust cycle, the next stage being asset bubbles (usually property and equities), over-investment and over-production, so further widening the gap between demand and supply. Such an economic system defies the purpose of democracy and social justice by any definition. Is this the kind of country which should be held up as an example to the rest of the world?

The answer has to be No because there are so many better countries deserving such a place. We might cite the Scandinavian or Benelux countries, the Far East Tigers, or France or Germany, as examples which come immediately to mind. The critique of America is that it is a power-crazed plutocracy, driven by the greed of making money out of money, or rentier profits, not so much for the gain of super-rich individuals, as to satisfy the impersonal interests of the money markets and a corporate system enslaving an entire population across the spectrum of society.

All human interests are sacrificed towards these ends. There is nothing wrong with profits if they are *directly* derived from tangibles or services of social value, or in fulfilling acceptable marketing demands, and are then ploughed back for reinvestment or used for the payment of reasonable dividends, taxation, etc.; but profits used predominantly for money creation lead inescapably to unsocial wealth accumulation, ongoing dispossession, and polarisation between an ever-richer but smaller class, and an expanding proportion of less affluent people. As work is necessarily central to our lives, it should be joyful and carried out with commitment to its specifically productive purpose; and as business is dependent on profits, the maximisation of *productive profitability*[29] should be sought in benefiting both commerce and the community.

But work should not be allowed to absorb every aspect of life (as it does in America) for then it becomes de-humanising. The individual has a right to himself, his family, and society, in maximising his personal fulfilment as an all-rounded being, and these needs are now recognised throughout Western Europe and in the Far East.

The mark of a civilised society is – and always has been – the need to use leisure wisely, not by slumping onto a sunbed in a sunny clime, or by frenzied touring through a dozen foreign lands in ten days; but by eating and drinking with friends, visiting art galleries, attending concerts, or by otherwise seeking to develop personal potential, both intellectually and spiritually. These are things which are either avoided or despised by the ethos of the American majority in favour of more synthetic pleasures such as feeding one-arm bandits in amusement arcades, lone drinking in bars, spectator sports, or indulging in video games. The American cannot tolerate anything which calls for reflection, stretches his imagination, or throws back a message for a personal response. Life is too fast for such painful demands and so he is only intent on escaping from himself through fantasy, games of chance, drink, or the disease of mindless acquisition.

15 – Enslavement through the unstoppable demands of an economic system

The American is not cursed with these traits because of intrinsic characteristics, but only because he is the victim of an economic system which drives him in these directions. The pressure to live at a speed beyond human endurance, and the pressure for ever greater economic growth, not only afflicts the well-being of the individual but is ultimately destructive to the economic system itself. The irony is that all these things are

---

[29] The economic implications of this have been examined in depth in my other books.

driven by the ideology of the financial-industrial set-up, and the
repudiation of measures to protect the planet, or reverse global
warming, are not so much motivated by the greed of the great
corporations as the necessity of assenting to the unstoppable
demands of the system. America is therefore riding a tiger from
which it cannot loosen its grip.

All this demonstrates the *loss* of freedom and not its gain,
since the individual, society, and the state have all surrendered
to forces beyond their control, and humanity is sacrificed in the
great whirlwind which unwittingly has been summoned up. And
no one (it seems) has the wit or courage to point the accusing
finger in analysing and denouncing the causes which have
brought this about. An intense and mindless belief in false idols
– and fear of the sin of doubt – maintains the self-sustaining
tyranny of the American economic system and the poison of its
global penetration.

And democracy, of course, has been turned on its head.
What hope is there for American humanity and the world
beyond? None, if the battle against ignorance is not launched
and won! All successful societies should have control over their
fate, but they only do so through an awareness of their
condition. No society on earth has ever had a lesser awareness
of its condition than America today. And here it has to be
acknowledged that the greater the technological complexity of a
society, then the greater are the demands on the mental powers
of its individual citizens in maintaining or furthering that level
of advancement.

And it is not sufficient that such a society be maintained
through the skills and energy of a small elite.   Advanced
industrial societies call on the cooperation of all through a high
level of educational attainment. And this attainment is not
restricted to practical skills or technological education, for
advanced societies are exposed to sudden and unanticipated
change, and these raise questions which are not merely practical
but philosophical. For example, the consequences of climate
warming or the depletion of fossil fuels, raise questions on how
we shall need to change our ways of living and attitudes to life.

These questions cannot be answered merely through the skills of a hands-on society, or by analysing the *as is* situation, but only through contemplating the *should be* questions for the future.

These are things which the common American mind is incapable of considering, and in this is to be found a major reason for the failure of their democracy. It is true that American education at the secondary level attempts to instil free thought and discussion, but it cannot hope to overcome two huge impediments: firstly, the unthinking conformism of American attitudes; and secondly, and more significantly, the emphasis on action and constant movement, in conjunction with a fast pace of life, which drives out the possibility for contemplation.

16 – America in need of an upward-inducing mobility

There has always existed an imbalance between liberty and equality in American political life which favours the former, but now there is a desperate need for a particular type of egalitarianism. This is not for a populist downward pulling egalitarianism, irrespective of whether this is seen in terms of Old Socialist proletarianism, or in terms of the patronising American pull to always meet the needs of the below average majority. The egalitarianism which is needed is one of upward-inducing mobility. It is not an egalitarianism motivated so much by the demands for a more equitable or just society, as an egalitarianism needed to facilitate a workable democracy.

A true democracy is dependent on positive as contrasted with negative voting, i.e. the electorate must vote for parties presenting policies in popular demand, and not merely for parties perceived as offering the lesser of several indifferent or bad alternatives. But a positive voting system cannot exist without an active intellectual life reaching all sectors of society, and this can only be achieved through higher educational standards with regard to understanding and discussing political theory and ideas touching many aspects of sociology and practical life. Educational systems approaching such standards are only now to be found in Germany, Scandinavia, France, and a handful of other countries. Amongst advanced industrial economies America is at the bottom of such an educational scale, and hence her democracy is the worst amongst countries claiming the benefits of freedom.

The idea that the majority should be highly educated in culture and the humanities is a new and revolutionary concept. In the past, from the time of the ancient Greeks until yesterday, it was an idea which was repudiated as both undesirable and impractical. It was undesirable because of class divisions, and the assumption that values and attitudes could not cross these barriers, except temporarily, in times of war. It was impractical because of the costs and time factors entailed in education, and the greater breadth of interests allowed to those with privilege, wealth, and leisure.

During the industrial period, those on the left were only interested in education in so far as it impacted on their political or revolutionary ends, and they encouraged the entrenchment of working class attitudes, since they valued solidarity above social advancement. But we now live in a world where, firstly, democracy can be made workable as a sound institution; and secondly, where society cannot hope to progress for the benefit of the majority, without the achievement of consistently high standards of education. And democracy, progress, and majority interests are interrelated concepts, interdependent on one another.

The future success of world freedom and democracy lies principally with the initiative of Europe and the Far East Tigers. A factor we have not touched upon, but nonetheless is highly significant, is that American democracy was hobbled by the four decades of the Cold War. All war is terrible in that convictions become entrenched and ideas for progress are paralysed during periods of conflict, and the Cold War was no exception. The Cold War was fought ideologically between two huge giants, and the rest of the world stood by feigning total or partial commitment to one side or the other, or otherwise becoming the unwitting victims of political entanglement, or worse. Early during this period the witch hunts of McCarthyism arose to ruin numberless individuals in both the government service and the arts, and the fear of Communists and liberals (both being associated with the other) remains until the present day, even though America emerged the clear victor of the Cold War in 1989.

17 – High culture as an aid to political consciousness

The fact that intellectuals such as Leo Strauss, Richard Perle, Irving Kristol, Francis Fukuyama, and more recently, Randy E. Barnett (right wing author of *The Structure of Liberty*), could assert or imply the end of history by proclaiming with fanatical conviction that the American way was the only way forward for the future of the planet, confirms the poverty of political ideas in America. The Cold War did irreparable damage to American intellectual life through instilling a culture of fear, suspicion, and hatred of the new, ambiguous, unknown, or allegedly incomprehensible, in the realm of political thought. But it went even further, for it killed off the possibility for political thought, when the latter became suspect as sin or deviation. The political conformism of America turned into arrogance, before mutating into determination to impose its dominance on the world.

The peoples of the democracies of the future need to be endowed with a greater breadth of knowledge and a high level of judgement. Political ability, as either an elector or politician (local or national), cannot be measured simply by an understanding of what politicians do or say, or by a careful reading of manifestos, or by studying the biographies of those standing for office, for all these are superficial things, and often of little guidance to what is *really* desirable or necessary for the future of society. It is necessary to understand the social sciences, and theories which underpin political principles and unite groups and drive them forward within a democratic framework.

It is for all these reasons that high culture must have a priority over low culture, in both education and sponsorship by either the state or business, or through national lotteries, not on the grounds that it is pre-eminent, but that it opens the way to a greater depth of understanding and perception. This is not to suggest that those who patronise high culture necessarily have a better judgement in political or other matters, but it certainly puts them at an advantage in developing their sensibility for forming a better judgement. Whilst the literary medium is certainly direct in raising the intellectual level of understanding, the high culture of music, painting, and the plastic arts, work in more subtle ways in developing thought and sensitivity of feeling.

The abysmal failure of American democracy may be summarised under the following headings:-

1. That the financial power of the plutocracy controls all the levers of political power;
2. That the media control public opinion through the great commercial corporations;
3. That the American people live under the deception of the pioneering ethos, and falsely believe that theirs is a "free" and "democratic" country;
4. That the illusions of Behaviourist psychological strategy is used in industry to satisfy employees in lieu of actual rights to co-determination or share-ownership;
5. That a debasing cultural populism and hedonistic attitudes have broken through the conventions of good taste, and are now assented to by the establishment as a control mechanism over the majority; and,
6. That the educational system unfits the majority in ensuring the survival of a sound democracy for the future.

18 – America is against majorities everywhere

Furthermore, America can no longer be correctly defined as a democracy on the following counts:-

1. Because there are no effective parties able to represent significant minorities, e.g. the poor, the unemployed, and those in low-paid jobs;
2. The practicalities of standing for election for the established parties is dependent on sponsorship from big business;
3. Employment carries no democratic rights as in most of the advanced industrialised world, with regard to co-determination, employee share-ownership, and often, trades union rights; and,
4. There is little or no protection for the poor or vulnerable in society with regard to sickness, unemployment, or old age benefits.

America is in reality a plutocracy driven by de-humanising forces characterised by the following:-

1. An economic system dependent on never-ending growth, and the maximisation of rentier profits, or the making of money out of money;
2. Money markets which are unpredictable or irrational, since they are beyond the decision-making of human control;
3. A frenetic work environment dictated by short-term pressures to ensure sufficient stock market returns, rather than the long-term purpose of maximising market share;
4. A money-oriented or business culture which penetrates every aspect of life;
5. A financial system which polarises wealth through a gradual process of dispossessing smaller owners in both the domestic and business spheres of activity;
6. Giant corporations which absorb the political establishment and then use it for their own purpose; and,
7. A financial-industrial juggernaut so powerful and omnipotent that it will stop at nothing in its path, even when confronted by environmental threats to the planet.

America has clearly set herself against the political will of the rest of the world with regard to the true principles of justice, equity, and democracy, especially as understood in Europe and the Far East. This is not to infer that injustice does not exist in other parts of the globe, but in the non-American world there is nonetheless an inevitable logic which is being pursued for a better life for majorities everywhere. This pursuit for justice is particularly exemplified through the legislation of the EU with regard to rights and obligations in maximising equality of opportunity. For the most part, this is honest legislation motivated by the purity of ethical concepts and a psychological understanding of the needs of the individual. It is for the most part uncorrupted by the vested interests of big business or particular groups in society with their own selfish agendas.

It is for these reasons that freedom and democracy are defined and understood for what they really mean, and not skewed to suit the political angle of powerful corporations. Hence an inevitable logic is followed with regard to working hours; minimum pay; decent holidays; child allowances; leave and employment protection following childbirth; free or subsidised education until degree level; free health services at the point of need; old age pensions matching three-quarters of last employment salary, etc. Americans will respond to the above with cynicism and horror, exclaiming, "But how can these things be paid for, and how can international competition be met at the same time?"

19 – Confronting the issues of price competition

Europeans fully acknowledge that competition is desirable – indeed essential – in maintaining choice, stimulating innovation, and ensuring the survival of the fittest products in maintaining the evolutionary spirit in industry; but they also realise that attempts to maintain international price competition against peoples in slave wage economies is a meaningless game. In America, the threat of international price competition is falsely used as an excuse for depressing wages, lengthening hours, and waiving other benefits. Such gestures, of course, do nothing to hold back the tide of competition as witnessed through the demise of manufacturing throughout the US, but they do help bolster share values and profits for investors and so further dividing rich and poor.

The European response of the EU, as well as that of other countries, is therefore wiser and more discerning. Why should nation states be obliged to cut back on reforms, social benefits, and living standards, which took centuries of struggle to achieve, in confronting the low exchange rates and minimal wages of competitor economies? Can any political or economic circumstances justify regression? The answer should always be No! Of course no country can be restricted in its economic policies in promoting its export efforts, but its target markets are equally entitled to respond by raising selective import controls in protecting the living standards of their peoples.

It should be borne in mind that America not only dominates the world financially and commercially in undermining socially beneficent economic systems, but hypocritically threatens the world, on moral and even charitable grounds, to maintain open markets as a strategy for survival. I use the term hypocritical without reservation since America has long been the most protectionist country on earth. For all these reasons, therefore, no country should be prepared to sacrifice its levels of achievement to the expediency of abstract economic principles, or to the forces of economies which threaten home-based industries, irrespective of whether those forces emanate from peoples enjoying relatively high living standards or linger on the borders of want.

Europe and the world are therefore intent on perfecting political systems according to majority needs, and uninfluenced by the intrusion of external vested interests. Political systems should be based on disinterested or objective principles, concerned only with the holistic needs of humanity. America can produce no intellectual response to these disinterested principles advanced by the rest of the world. She repudiates the consideration of questions of right and wrong on the grounds that they are impractical; arguing instead that free market forces and the power of money alone should direct the fate of humanity.

She uses the moral argument of Adam Smith in supporting such a stance, viz., that trust should be placed in the Invisible Hand of God – although Smith never referred directly to the name of the deity. Furthermore, if this great economist could see the way in which his principles are perverted by contemporary America, he would turn in his grave. In the 21st century an anachronistic interpretation is given to *The Wealth of Nations*, a book which was written as a plea against the mercantilism and impossible restrictions of 18th century trade. We now live in a world which bears no comparison with that of the 18th century, and we are now confronted by immense social and environmental problems which never existed before, and they cry out for state intervention on a massive scale.

20 – America does not carry the emblem of ideal modernity

We must return to a topic we touched upon briefly early in the previous chapter. It is often argued that what we criticise or most dislike about the American way of life, or American institutions, or the American mode of capitalism, is nothing more nor less than an *essential* symptom of modernity. This is a lie, and it is a lie which must be repudiated definitively. America and everything she represents is in origin specific to that country alone. Of course the American influence is experienced worldwide, and inescapably, accompanying that influence will be all the malign characteristics of her culture, but it is quite fallacious to conclude that such characteristics are intrinsic to modernity.

If, for example, America had never existed, modernity would have taken quite a different route. Modes of business, social attitudes, and styles of living, now everywhere taken for granted would never have come into existence. Instead, Europe and other countries further afield, would have developed different and better cultures. It is a strong probability that a debasing populism and the dragging down of standards would never anywhere have occurred.

Due to the forces of Social or Productive capitalism emanating from Continental Europe and the Far East, and the global repercussions of this, more egalitarian societies would have emerged everywhere, and influenced by the attitudes of a predominantly middle class culture, higher standards would have been achieved in education and all other spheres of existence. There would have been a slower pace of life, and more meaningful leisure activities in closer keeping with the spiritual needs of humanity.

Political life would have been more sophisticated and less confrontational, for freed from the economic divisiveness of American capitalism, left/right conflictual patterns would have withered in favour of the representation of functional groups jostling gently at a simmer for marginal advantages on a spate of issues. This would have reflected the working of democracy at its best, and the enjoyment of civilised values would have predominated throughout every sector of a society which was fair, equitable, and at peace with itself.

Such a society would therefore have been far in advance of that which we find today. In working for a better future, and in understanding modernism as it *should be* and not as it *has* been, it is necessary for the non-American world to unify its interests against the forces of barbarism and self-destruction. And let there be no doubt that the American system *is* self-destructive, for it is bound on a course which has set in place impersonal mechanisms which are irreversible, and mindlessly driving the world towards both economic and environmental catastrophe. Leading thinkers in government departments throughout the world talk in hushed tones about the bubble which is destined to burst in the dark Winter of a not-to-distant future.

Efforts to avoid such a catastrophe become the duty of us all according to the limited capacities at our individual disposal. America must be confronted – for the sake of her own people, as well as that of any other. If the non-American world has sufficient faith in the values of civilisation, then civilisation may be saved. But we must strengthen our vision for the way ahead, and plan boldly for a more intelligent and humane society. Without such conviction, and without the will to achieve, there can be little hope for the future of humankind.

****

CHAPTER 5

A GLOBAL STRATEGY FOR THE PLANET AND HUMANKIND

"Climate change and a looming crunch in the supply of our principal energy source, oil, are set to revolutionise energy systems. The choices we make in the next few years will either set us on a path to economic and environmental chaos or lay the foundations of a resilient, sustainable and sociable way to meet our energy needs."

Andrew Sims, "Our Best is not good enough," *New Statesman* supplement, 3rd October 2005, p. iv.

1 – America's irresponsibility to the world community

Within three weeks of John Bolton, George W. Bush's appointee as the American ambassador to the United Nations taking up his post in August 2005, he had demanded no less than 750 amendments to the blueprint, originally drafted by the UN Secretary General, Kofi Annan, restating the ideals of the international body. The amendments were spelt out in a 32-page US version, first reported by the *Washington Post* and then acquired and published by *The Independent* on 26th August.

The leading points behind these amendments may be summarised as follows:- with regard to *Poverty*, the US sought to delete from the blueprint reference to the UN's Millennium Goals, tackling poverty and disease; with regard to *Aid*, removal of agreed targets to poor nations; with regard to *Climate change*, the scrapping of provisions calling for action to halt global warming; with regard to *Nuclear weapons*, the scrapping of provisions calling on nuclear powers to speed up disarmament; with regard to *Trade*, restriction on Third world countries joining the World Trade Organisation, and with regard to the *International Criminal Court*, deletion of its reference as the world's permanent war crimes court.

This extraordinary intervention by America's representative, which has dismayed so many other delegates at the UN, is clearly intended as a contemptuous insult to the world's forum for progress, but it is much more than that. Not only is it an unwarranted intrusion into the constructive efforts of a supposedly disinterested body for a better future, but it is a slap in the face for the peoples of the world. Furthermore, it is a mischievous meddling which actually throws a spanner into the dedicated and good work of many professional organisations comprising the UN in the struggle to resolve the most intractable problems confronting both humanity and the future of the planet.

It is not insignificant that within days of the US published Amendments, that the southern States of America were struck by the Katrina hurricane, bringing destruction in its wake over an area larger than the size of Britain. The impact of the disaster was on a scale which suggested that this was something altogether different in its origins from the customary storms at that period of the year. The scale of the disaster suggested that climate warming could not be excluded as a contributory factor, and yet the financial-industrial establishment, together with the administration, still insists that there is no such thing as an environmental threat to our planet. And the reason for this mulish stance is explained in the previous chapter.

America is the most powerful country on earth, and yet at the same time, she is also the most irresponsible. It seems as if every action she takes in the international field is not merely doomed to failure, but doomed to explode in disaster with repercussions which could never have been predicted. Furthermore, she is incapable of learning anything from her litter of mistakes left across the face of the globe. Where she has intended to plant democracy, she has only created tyranny; where she has acted to generate prosperity, she has only left poverty, famine, and disease; and where she has sought to make peace, she has evoked new conflicts, war, and terrorism in their wake. Two causes alone have been responsible for this ongoing catastrophe: firstly, the false and self-destructive ideology of

Rentier capitalism, as outlined in the first chapter of this book; and secondly, the crass ignorance of the men and women who wield power in the United States.

2 – The consequences of absolute power

As we have noted earlier in this book, America does have the largest and best research institutes in the social sciences, and many of the best thinkers in this sphere of knowledge, but none of the good work produced by these academics is capable of making a significant impact on the financial-industrial establishment which holds the levers of power. America is not a place where reason is allowed to reign. Only the rude bully is allowed to exert any sway on issues which really matter. The spirit of Al Capone is far closer to the business of American government than the idea of a benevolent despot. This explains, therefore, not only the utter contempt with which America regards the United Nations, but the utter contempt with which she views all the countries of the planet.

In view of the above remarks, we must nonetheless remain sufficiently realistic to recognise that *all* politics is concerned with the exertion of power, and that any individual who fails to heed the intelligent philosophy of Machiavelli, places him- or herself and his country at grave risk of defeat or destruction. Now America currently occupies a situation of might in the international sphere which has *never* been enjoyed by any European power. She is a foremost economic and military power without rivals to challenge her supremacy. This contrasts sharply with dominating European powers over the past four centuries, i.e. Spain, France, Britain, Russia, Prussia, or Austria-Hungary, for all these countries at the time of their pre-eminence were always constrained within a balance of power situation. And this is no longer the case with the US in the post-Cold War era.

Consequently, America is able to adopt an absolutist attitude with regard to perceived hindrances emanating from any country on earth – and despite the privilege of enjoying overwhelming power, she is still disturbed by a thousand minor irritants from many nation states across the globe. These irritants usually concern restrictive trade practices, or its opposite, the dumping of cheap goods. It is because American power is directly financial-industrial, as opposed to being mediated and socialised through representative systems, that she remains hyper-sensitive to all questions touching on trade and business.

No other country on earth is so sensitive to these matters, or reacts with such violent retaliatory measures when her vested interests are touched. Whilst other countries would be perceived as endangered by the worst economic crises, if they responded in the same way to similar conditions, America, it has to be assumed, is merely motivated by greed. Whilst the non-American world is accustomed to receiving knocks and difficulties in the realm of barter and exchange as the natural course of events, America, it seems, has not yet developed sufficient maturity to endure the smallest slight to her sensibility.

And this tendency is exacerbated rather than diminished by her present status. America sees no reason to yield in the slightest to any nation state, be it great or small. She has no need for constraint and nothing will restrain her. The all-powerful are unchallengeable and absolute. The appeal to magnanimity on her part would be dismissed as an absurdity. As far as she is concerned the idea of magnanimity is a convenient fiction invented by the weak in ensuring a more compliant attitude from the strong. It is not suggested here that this political ruthlessness stems from the intrinsic characteristics of the American people. It is argued, on the contrary, that this ruthlessness stems solely from the accidental possession of power in itself, for as the great historian, Lord Acton, remarked a hundred years ago, "power corrupts and absolute power corrupts absolutely."

This is not to imply that overt bullying is the invariable tactic of American administrations. In following the precept of her most jingoistic President, Theodore Roosevelt, she prefers to "walk quietly with a big stick," and use the subtlety of public relations and deceptive advertising. As we noted in an earlier chapter, this is how she promotes her insidious form of Rentier capitalism throughout the nations of the world. She simply buys up business, wherever it may be bought, and then transforms the nature of the capitalist process before the vendors have awoken to the consequences.

This form of *conquest* is closer to the methods of a Trojan-worm or computer virus than to the *William* of the same name. When society then asks what became of the social democratic consensus, and the social capitalism, which achieved so much in the decades of the post-War period in Europe and the Far East, the answer comes back that "that form of capitalism is no longer viable!" How fittingly such an answer fulfils the exploitative needs of the great American corporations! And how credulous are the peoples who so easily accept the great lie! The conquest of American capital was so quietly achieved, and so unresistingly, that it went unnoticed, and when good systems were defeated, they were ignorantly dismissed as unviable and belonging to the past. This was the work of the true Trojan-worm.

3 – Confronting America is an ethical imperative

The greater truth, of course, is that America is as much a threat to herself as to the rest of the world. She is no less a part of the planet than any other nation, and will suffer in no lesser degree from Rentier corporations and climate change and their consequences. Her people must be aware of the terrible threats which lie ahead. Perhaps she is suffering from a form of intellectual repression in the face of dangers with which she might be confronted.

Perhaps her hyper-sensitivity to trade matters is symptomatic of this psychological repression. After all, her wild adventures in Vietnam, Somalia, Afghanistan, Iraq, and numerous other territories throughout the globe, are doomed eventually to drive her into the ground. The costs of modern warfare are greater relatively today than they have ever been before. The wealth of the mightiest powers remains finite in the last resort. And one fact is certain, if no other: America is a country which is obsessed with fear, and this shows through all her bluster, arrogance and humbug.

In any event it has now become imperative that America should be challenged – and challenged by all the peoples and nations of the world. This is because America is set on a disaster course for us all, and set on the rails of an ideology which is false and self-destructive, and from which she is incapable of changing direction – and no government and no sector of the American population is capable of applying the brakes before the train finally hits the buffers ahead.

How can such a challenge be mounted? It would be futile simply to produce a rational critique analysing the false thinking and wrong policies of the American administration, or on the ills of the power-wielding corporations, and how they have expropriated the function of government. Such intellectualising would be like water over a duck's back, and would be lost in no time in the bottomless pit of political argumentation. It would be so ineffective as not even to draw a gesture of dismissal, or the batting of an American eyelid.

Furthermore, the problems of American capitalism are complex and technical, and not easily designed to arouse the imagination of ordinary men and women, who are impatient of the idea in needing to comprehend the mechanics of economic and industrial systems. And yet, if these problems are to be addressed, and if politics is to have any verity, they are difficulties which must be discussed and placed at the forefront of political thinking and political action.

But as we have said, if politics is not about the exertion of power, it becomes a *nothingness*. If the truth is to be upheld, there must be no watering down of principles or intentions. How then can public opinion be aroused and directed without compromising the truth behind these difficult issues? In achieving *Realpolitik* these are principles which need to be *personalised*, so they are transformed into concrete issues which are easily understood by the majority. In this way the imagination of the majority may be aroused and utilised for a great moral crusade in furthering the cause of worldwide humanity. There is no other means by which these vital issues may be politicised, and it is their ethical content which makes imperative the need for *Realpolitik*.

4 – Political justification for anti-Americanism

These are the reasons why the launching of a worldwide campaign against America is not merely imperative, but inescapable as the most rational strategy in confronting the intractable problems of our time. This is because resistance to the greatest evils now facing planet earth are stopped in their tracks by the financial-industrial power and administration of the United States government. These evils may be listed as:-

1. A malign economic system undermining the social capitalism of Europe and the Far East;
2. A political-military imperialism undermining the integrity of predominantly Third world states, and preventing the formation of democratic government;
3. The cultural domination of peoples and countries throughout the world, resulting in the denigration of values for the advancement of humankind; and,
4. Refusal to acknowledge environmental threats to the planet, or to take necessary measures for regeneration, or to cut back on the exhaustion of fossil fuels, or to innovate and invest in self-sustainable energy resources.

How would the *personalisation* of these issues be exactly presented? It would clearly entail the condemnation of a country and its people conceived as generalities. That is, as the above evils clearly emanate from the cited country and its population, and are manifested throughout the world, the condemnation is justified as both a natural response and defensive tactic against unwarranted attack.   As the condemnation arises from the existence of general rather than universal tendencies, it would *not* entail discrimination against all individuals in the said countries, although certainly a reminder to all of the situation as it is seen.

Such condemnation of an entire people for their collective guilt would call for a wariness of all individuals but not the need for unpleasantness or incivility. The hope would always be borne in mind for an eventual change of political conditions leading to reconciliation and the return of friendly relations – but such a change would be a distant rather than a sooner prospect. This is because all the alleged evils stem not simply from political or economic causes, but from cultural characteristics deeply embedded in the nature of the people, and so a desirable transformation could not reasonably be expected within a short time-span.

There are practical virtues to be found in asserting all major political ills as the responsibility of a single people, providing in the first place, the facts are established as valid. Firstly, the issues are concretised at their source, and are simplified for the comprehension of the majority. Not only are they clarified, but they take on an emotive power, as loathing is directed at symbols which are already objects of ridicule or hatred. By this means abstract or difficult economic concepts are given meaning or sense to a majority which could never have grasped them in any other way.

Secondly, the scapegoating of a people must arouse its conscience, and set in motion doubt, and trigger questions as to its underlying beliefs and modes of behaviour and action. The targeting of America with a list of accusations on matters of equity or justice or the environment, must draw a response, and hopefully, would lead to change. Politicians would be subject to questioning and pressure from their electors, and if the non-American world was to follow up verbal criticism with trade embargoes, or worse, the American administration might even be forced to confront the corporations with serious legislation, as once occurred with the Anti-trust laws of 100 years ago.

Thirdly, and most significantly, the concentrating of ills as blameable on a single nation by the world community, would help unite the peoples of the world towards a common purpose.

A spirit of amity would develop amongst the most diverse peoples as they discovered a unifying bond against a common foe, and differences which had been divisive hitherto would fall away. The need to stamp out American cultural domination in upholding national integrity, would leave room for re-discovering the cultures of smaller nation states, and this would lead to the renaissance of declining arts and industries, and a greater exchange amongst the countries of the world.

Fourthly, and lastly, such a political perspective of the world's ills would contribute towards a more objective approach to problems. As noted in the opening chapter of this book, the evolutionary development of society and the world of work in the advanced industrialised world has outlived the bankrupt ideologies of the past. There is now no longer any credibility in the clash of class-based politics, and this is the *sole* reason for the collapse of party political memberships of all hues throughout the developed world.

5 – A pattern for a more creative politics

Established parliamentary movements are no longer able to attract first-rate minds for their leadership as was once the case in the Victorian period or early in the 20th century. Political party activists across the spectrum of left/right thinking are only able to attract third-rate minds. They are too often those who are *professional* or *career* politicians with little experience in the university of life, and hence are only those who are on the make for their own financial gain. This sad situation and decline of democracy has occurred because society has reached a developmental stage whereby it feels a deep distaste for any politics which seeks to attract voters according to their economic or social status. Left/right politics is discredited and done for! It is no longer capable to advancing the democratic process.

The real problems which face us today transcend the issues of class, and this is sensed by every intelligent man or woman throughout Europe, the Far East, and further afield. The democracy of the future will need to be based on the representation of functional groups. The politics of single issue movements may be strong whilst party politics sits in the doldrums, but national or international politics appealing to the conscience and unity of all must ultimately be based on national parliamentary movements. That is, *governing* parties, whether local or national, must be based on *broadly general* as opposed to *narrowly specific* principles. And this is the problem which faces us today.

How can we extricate ourselves from the curse of class-based politics which in today's society is hindering the resolution of substantive issues rather than resolving them – if not actually compounding them? It is necessary to adopt an entirely new perspective of the political landscape if politics is again to become creative and democratic. This returns us to the question of *Realpolitik* and the practical need to motivate majorities towards desired ends.

If collective blame is passed onto America for the ills which afflict the peoples of the world today, then the citizens of every other nation state, irrespective of their economic or social standing, may sit down in goodwill as equals, and without embarrassment to one another, and rationally set-about the resolution of the problems confronting them. In such an assembly for debate, where all are drawn through good intent towards a more common purpose, a spontaneous environment will be created for a deeper and more objective consideration of issues.

In such an assembly, freed from the old internal suspicions and distrust of class-based opponents, there will emerge the unabashed candour and energy and time for easily formulating desirable practical policies. This is because the enmity to be confronted will be an external foe, and not something to frustrate the internal mechanisms of parliamentary procedures. A similar situation would pertain in the international sphere, where representatives of the most diverse countries would gather in a spirit of friendship and common understanding in cooperating for a mutual purpose.

6 – Moving from a class-based to an internationally-based politics

The prime purpose justifying a campaign for freedom from America is therefore to be found in the catalyst it will generate in creating a new and better politics worldwide. Americans may baulk at the idea of their country being used as a springboard for a new and better politics for justice and equity, but it should be borne in mind that the use is intended as pointing to a metaphor rather than to an intrinsic reality.

That is, it is the values of America which raise such an objection in the mind of the non-American world, and not the separate individuals of which it is composed, each of whom must be considered on his or her own merits. The bad or typically conceived general characteristics of the American individual cannot be applied as a blanket description of *all* Americans, and hence exceptions must be allowed to prove the rule.

Furthermore, it is not intended that America or Americans should be exposed to ridicule or contempt from now until the end of time. After all, they are human like the rest of us, and as humans subject to change and reformation. These facts we are bound to bear in mind in the name of equity and fairness. It is anticipated that many Americans will support the underlying moral principles outlined in this book, even if they take exception to the methods for promoting them. Those Americans with a more liberal frame of mind, or a greater awareness of the outside world, those from the East coast or California, are more likely to be attracted by the truths we have attempted to convey.

It is the peoples of the Midwest, the deep South, and the bigots of the Bible belt, who will be most difficult to persuade and bring to reason. It is these latter who insist that the ills of the world are always explicable to Man's original sin, and that therefore a helping hand for the poor and oppressed is a kind of defiance against God's will. It is these who will insist until the day of Armageddon, that climate warming or environmental deterioration has nothing to do with the excessive burning of fossil fuels, or extravagant living styles, but is solely accountable to God's anger at the sins of humankind. Their answer to all the problems of poverty, disease, famine, and misery, is not the application of intelligent measures (unless they happen to coincide with bringing a usurious return on invested capital) but the power of *prayer*.

It is unfortunate that it is these people who dominate the thinking and decision-making of modern America, and it is in them that is to be found the greatest evil on our planet today. It is the superstitions of the flat-earthers, the creationists, and the "intelligent designers," that the non-American world needs to confront in the present age. And it is for these reasons that we need not make any apology in launching a campaign against America and her so-called civilisation.

The primary reason calling for the transformation of our perspective of the political landscape from a class-based outlook to an international view of issues, stems from the fact that the major problems worrying peoples today *are* indeed international, and cannot be intelligibly addressed through a class-based mindset. This is self-evident with regard to environmental issues, equally affecting all sectors of humanity, and requiring cooperation between nations rather than between conflicting vested interest groups. But it equally applies to confronting the ills of Neo-American or Rentier capitalism, which, in its complexity and manifestations, transcends the quarrelsome comprehension of conflicting status groups in society.

As we have argued elsewhere at length: firstly, contemporary corporate capitalism cannot be properly identified as controlled or owned by a clearly identifiable class; and secondly, it has a logic and impetus of its own beyond the control of those who are nominally responsible for its outcome. And this, especially with regard to the money markets, is what makes Rentier capitalism so frightening to the majority. It offers the first *real* example of machines taking over from people, i.e., the fast-moving medium of information technology promotes a process, the consequences of which are unknown from day-to-day, and cannot be controlled by human will.

7 – National interests only achievable through international cooperation

All these environmental, economic, and political problems which are currently undermining the good efforts of governments worldwide – and are therefore more than merely threats – are not only beyond the scope of classes to resolve, but of nations also, even when they muster all their resources for the purpose. The single nation which applies all the best principles for a self-sustainable environment is merely whistling in the wind if few are influenced by its example. And no nation can any longer control its economic destiny, nor even formulate an economic policy in any real sense, when confronted by the might of the American dollar.

Hence any state which wishes to uphold its economic or cultural integrity must cooperate internationally to achieve such aims. And since it is America alone which is the economic force frustrating the achievement for the independence of nations and peoples worldwide, it follows that America is the power against which the rest of the world must unite. What other political alternative remains? Only total surrender to the ruinous dictates of the most powerful nation on earth.

The imperative of launching an anti-American campaign is not because of anti-Americanism *per se*, but because of the need to create equity and justice for all the people of the planet. When I and other social scientists first sought to define the foundations for justice and equity, we explored the facts of sociology and examined the principles of social ethics, without any thought of political ideologies or particular nation states.

But when we came to applying our conclusions to the real world, we were forced to look at the present actualities of power politics, and very quickly we came to realise that the peoples and nations of the world were cornered by the great bully of America. What, then, was the non-American world to do? There was only one thing it could do – must do, and that was to regain its own space by fighting its way out of the corner. The struggle against America, therefore, is the one and only *practical* path in achieving the freedom of the non-American world – and ultimately, of America also.

How is the new politics of Social capitalism and justice and equity to be achieved through the campaign for freedom from America? In a certain sense the new politics is almost upon us. Never has America been more discredited than it is today. Intuitively, thinking men and women in Europe and throughout the world already realise the bankruptcy of the old parties, and the need for new ideas in regenerating democracy. They are sickened by the old slogans, false labels, the spin-doctoring and hypocrisy of the dying politics of today. A new brand of men and women are needed – more imaginative, intelligent, better informed and perceptive than those who have gone before – to take up the torch of the new enlightenment.

Those who are politically active today and committed to the bankrupt ideologies across the spectrum of left/right thinking, supposedly representing the peoples of Europe and beyond, in parliaments throughout the world, must be knocked off their perch of certainties in confronting the new realities. But how are they to be awoken and made aware of these realities? Hardly by the power of words, or a book such as the present publication! Through long experience in political life I have long since learnt that rank and file political activists are not thinking people, and they rarely, if ever, read a book on political theory.

The ideas which they hold, attributable to political or socio-economic thinkers, are usually received at third or fourth hand, and even then, in a garbled fashion. Therefore, the thinker intent on motivating people to adopt sound ideas on justice and equity for the betterment of humankind must achieve more than merely defining the parameters for an ethically and economically desirable society. He must also prepare a catalyst for bringing such ideas into fruition. And that is the function of a campaign for freedom from America.

8 – Anti-Americanism is the creative radical politics of the future

In a former era, when society was very different from what it is today, when peoples were clearly divided by separate class interests, radicals and Socialist thinkers called for revolution as a means for achieving the just society. Revolution was never an end in itself but a means for arousing publicity to current ills through demonstrations and marches; for stimulating constructive thought; and finally, for knocking the establishment off its perch. But the idea of calling for revolution today is a crass absurdity. The divisions between poor and rich *in terms of owning assets* may be as great, or greater today, than in earlier epochs, but in all other respects, the interrelationships binding people across every sector of society in advanced industrial economies, are so complex, that any kind of revolution would be of equal hurt to all and of benefit to none.

Throughout Western Europe, and the peninsular and island-based Tiger economies, the effects of taxation, welfare, pension investment policies, mortgage and loan arrangements, banking and fiscal policies in promoting full employment and sound business, are so delicately balanced and so interdependent on one another, that the very idea of revolution would be irresponsible and anarchic, and wholly catastrophic in its outcome. Hence there has to be an alternative to revolution in effecting desired political and social change.

If society is unable to advance, it atrophies and degenerates, and hardens into a living-death, as China before 1912 or Turkey before 1923. Already the first signs of degeneration are made evident in the advanced industrial economies: firstly, as witnessed through the poverty of new political thinking; secondly, as witnessed through the failure of parliamentary movements to keep apace with technological and social change; and thirdly, because the rational desires of the majority of thinking but politically uncommitted people are no longer represented in any positive fashion. It should be noted that the so-called *apathetic majority* nonetheless hold heartfelt political views on many issues. We live in an age of information overload and the spewing out of endless statistics, and many are mistakenly deceived that this is sufficient in lieu of new ideas, but of course it is not.

Mere factual information, cooked-up by political aides or so-called Personal Secretaries, is too often used by politicians in blinding the public with "science," but mere facts are just empty dross if not utilised within the framework of creative ideas in meeting the future. And since our democratic institutions are failing in their purpose, and since the prospect of revolution is no longer a desirable option, where can we turn in regenerating democratic political life? The necessary catalyst can only be found through launching a political campaign against America and everything she represents – even if in the mêlée which follows, some good gets accidentally knocked over together with the bad.

The reasons morally justifying such a campaign have been elaborated above in the greater part of the book. The reason of expediency for such a campaign is that the entire non-American world loathes America and her people, for a host of motives. The reason for such a campaign is not because we dislike America, but because we dislike injustice and inequity. The immediate response to such a campaign would be to arouse the curiosity of the majority, in instigating such questions as, Why,? and, To what extent do I agree with the accusations alleged? This in turn leads to an identity of thinking, and anger, followed quickly by a desire for more information to confirm old prejudices and acquire *new knowledge.*

And it is in the acquisition of new knowledge that the real value of the campaign is to be sought. It is here where the constructive part of our politico-economic philosophy is to be found. But without the shock tactics of a campaign of loathing against America, and the subsequent stages of response, it would be impossible to introduce the majority to the political implications of our time with all their financial-industrial complexity. It is the sole way of advancing social progress.

How else can new ideas be introduced? How else can discussion be stimulated in planning reforms for the future?

9 – The call for a more intelligent political class

It may be suggested: But why not link in with existing parliamentary groups to the left of centre, on important issues, and in such circles arouse discussion? The answer, sadly, is that the complexity of these issues is beyond their comprehension for intelligent discussion. The knowledge base is simply just not there. All the great trades unions have their research officers and reference libraries, and every member of parliament has his/her personal assistant with his nose permanently pressed against a computer screen or up against a volume of statistics, but none of this seems to help towards a better understanding of our underlying problems. This is possibly because ideas are still fixed ideologically in a past age. Prejudice must reign in supporting notions fixed in our grandfather's era, and so all research is used for what is "already known."

There was a time when I thought the unions were moving into a new age, and a *reactive* movement was becoming *proactive* with regard to the re-organisation and success of industry. When John Monks took over the TUC there were plans for "partnership" and cooperation, and high hopes for the future; but now that his term is over, there is regression and talk of return to an era of conflict and strikes.

Meanwhile, fine sounding states(wo)men and other politicians, all of whom have their speeches written for them (and are ignorant of the very matters on which they speak so authoritatively) are soon uncovered as unscrupulous charlatans. Why is this? It is because the interests of those who are left of centre are predominantly committed to questions of redistribution or public welfare, and they have little interest or time or capacity for understanding the mechanics of business or finance or social wealth creation. This may present a dismal picture of our political establishment, but from my personal observation and experience, it is entirely true.

In this is to be found the argument for bringing into existence an entirely new political class. The old divisive politics is failing our civilisation, and its remnants are hindering thought and serious reform in every direction. The left/right parties, with their discredited ideologies, should disband and go now – if only they had the notion and will to do so! But what should replace them? Who should be elected as the politicians and statesmen of the future? In view of the complexity of the financial-industrial systems of the advanced industrial economies, there are two sets of qualities which are urgently sought: the first is concerned with technical ability; and the second is concerned with ideological commitment, and the two must always work in tandem.

With regard to technical ability, the rulers and politicians of the future must be hand-picked from amongst the most experienced and knowledgeable in the business community, spread equally amongst bankers, financiers, manufacturers, accountants, scientists, engineers, and international traders, etc. They must be mature people with hands-on experience in different spheres of activity, with firm convictions on those processes which best benefit the community. Since it is the activity of the business community which ultimately always directs the material living standards of us all, it is commonsense that they should be closest to the levers of real power, providing that the mechanisms of the business process are socialised in serving the interests of the community.

When we call upon the more educated to take up the reins of political power, we are not only referring to those with a string of academic degrees, for these in themselves are often meaningless dross. Political ability is not amenable to the restraints of organised knowledge presented within a straitjacket, for the reason that legislation defies the past and needs to anticipate the future. Politics calls for a very special intuitive sense and a distinctive creative imagination. The knowledge basis for this, therefore, must be considerable but undefined. The qualities that are needed are those of self-education rather than imposed-education, i.e. an education received through the university of life.

A hundred years ago, there were many highly-educated (or well-read) working class people in the labour movement. They were self-educated with no degrees from any school or college, and because of this, they were competent in the business of the politics of their time. Today such people do not exist in any number. This is because the restraints of formal education in the social sciences has tended to hobble the visionary approach of the greater picture of politics, and so too, the power of appealing to a wider public. In addition, we live in an age of dumbed-down universal further education, when those who look to broadening their outlook, set themselves within a rigid framework to acquire it, and dare not allow their curiosity to randomly choose a book for this purpose if it is not already on an *approved reading list*. This is symptomatic of the debasement of our intellectual life today!

With regard to ideological commitment, it should be acknowledged that business needs to be organised and managed for the longer term. Its rationale should be for the maximising of market share and the stability of the enterprise for its own productive purpose. The commitment of employees should be encouraged through schemes for co-determination and employee share-ownership, and not merely through Taylorism or the trickery of Behaviourist psychology. After a long career in industry, I see no problem in drawing the majority of business people in the advanced industrialised non-American world to adopting such ideas with enthusiasm. Indeed, the adoption of such ideas is going to be essential for the survival of manufacturing in Europe and the Far East in the years ahead.

10 – Enlightened business magnates and the mantle of power

Of course the adoption of such ideas remains anathema to American corporate thinking. As the rationale of American business is solely the maximisation of investors' profits, employees are merely fodder who may be used or disposed of as need arises, with no thought for their future or family circumstances. Although the virtues of Fordism originally brought wages higher than the average in American industry, the majority of American industrial workers are now paid little above legally minimum earnings.

The cash nexus alone unites employer and worker, and this facilitates a casual hire and fire mentality, and an environment of instability throughout the majority of organisations. The concentration on investors' profits is also a self-destructive philosophy, for not only does it entail a game of musical chairs within conglomerates, but the struggle to keep down wages is also matched by resistance to invest in the latest automotive technologies, and this is the reason why America has lost out to Japan over recent decades.

Although fifty years ago such attitudes were in part accepted by much of industry in the non-American world, there is now a very different mode of thinking. In the immediate post-War era, the condescension of patriarchal attitudes could accommodate aspects of US management policy, but with the transformation of society over recent decades, we now live in a very different world. In meeting and speaking with leading British and German industrialists in a purely social (i.e. non-political) context over the past two or three years, and listening to their anxieties and precepts for the future, I have encountered an outlook which is rarely reflected in the media.

It certainly puts the lie to the stereotypical picture of industrialists as imagined or portrayed by those supporting left of centre movements, but then the stereotypical image is probably fixed as that of the typical American corporate chief executive. It may be true that those industrialists I've encountered are not representative of the majority of their class, but they are those at the top of their profession, successful, and at the peak of their careers, and they are educated and cultured men with a broad vision of society. Almost invariably they have strong political opinions whilst holding no allegiance to any particular group.

Again and again I have heard the following views: that the funding of industry should be based on a more stable system; that the state should exert a positive initiative in promoting home-based manufacturing; that greater investment should be made in scientific research and technological investment; that a country no longer producing tangibles is placing its international financial services sector at risk of extinction; that the production of tangibles, or primary industries, *must* remain the driving force for wealth creation in the majority of economies; that in the modern age with its educated middle-middle majority, you cannot pull the wool over the eyes of socially-aware employees; that honesty and open relationships are always the best course in securing the longer term loyalty of workers; and, that co-determination (*Mitbestimmung*) and employee share-ownership is by far the best strategy for industrial efficiency and the success of the enterprise.

It is such men and women who should be drawn into the heart of our political system – even if they have to be cajoled against their will. Industrialists are generally those who seldom aspire to political office, but lack of ambition is rarely a disqualification in the world of politics. It may be noted that in a past age – in the Victorian era – it was often those with least ambition – who needed to be persuaded against the odds to take up the reigns of power – who proved to be the wisest and most effective statesmen.

Those of great wealth, who enjoy the quiet leisure of a country existence, and yet are scholarly and experienced in the ways of the world, often possess the characteristics of the finest rulers, since they have a disinterested attitude towards issues, care little about what others think of them, and use a cool and fair judgement in decision-making. Democracy is fortunate when it chooses those without ambition to represent its interests, as it then succeeds in excluding spin-doctors, corrupt politicians on the make, compulsive liars, and other such demagogues who eventually earn the contempt of the majority.

The best industrialists amongst us are as socially concerned about the welfare and future of the general population to no lesser degree than those who aspire to left wing ideologies or support their representing parliamentary movements. It should be noted that a businessman may cherish all the socially-aware sentiments expressed by *The Guardian* without even needing to read that paper. In other words, the established left does not by any means hold a monopoly in the promotion of social justice and equity.

11 – How business leaders will succeed where Socialists failed

The attitude of industrialists in Europe and the Far East is in sharp contrast to that very different breed in America with its loud-mouthed ambitions to take over the world. More worthy of emulation than the square-jawed American businessman with his boasting and arrogance, and assertion that in dynamism he is second to none, is the Japanese industrial mogul with his self-effacement and polite demeanour, who prefers to spend his leisure hours by meditating quietly in a temple garden, rather than playing the peacock before friends by a game of squash. And which of these is the more successful, and which is a greater credit to the community? It is the Japanese, who through his quiet energy conquers the world, whilst his American counterpart flits from one organisation to another, generating, through guile, sufficient profits to satisfy investors, but achieving little in terms of producing tangibles or social capital.

It has to be said, however, that those to the left of centre have always been suspicious of the motives of the business community with regard to their participation in political life. This, of course, has been due to the old divide between capital and labour which for so long has been seen as unbridgeable. It has also been due, as noted above, to the reluctance of those to the left of centre to comprehend the world of business and high finance, and how the mechanics of the latter actually impacts on the life of ordinary people. The narrow vision of the left has only been concerned with re-distribution and welfare, and in terms of understanding society in its entirety, this is like attempting to cure disease without having any notion of its causes.

As most the ills of society stem from the malfunctioning of the economy through the activity of business, so most the benefits of the economy are experienced through the successful functioning of business. The failure of left of centre governments has always been due to the failure of economic policy to understand or cooperate with business in a desirable way, or to fall into the trap of introducing policies which conflict with the needs of business. Left of centre governments in democratic societies have generally been contented with leaving business to manage its own affairs subject to legislative tinkering at the edges in promoting welfare, health and safety, employment rights, and insurance for sickness and old age.

But the time has now arrived when such a limited approached by government is failing to satisfy the heavy demands and problems of the future. The time is fast approaching when it will be necessary for government to take a far more proactive stance in stimulating wealth creation and business success than hitherto. This may sound suspiciously like a call for Old Socialist measures, but nothing of the kind is intended. Yes, there will be a call for industry to better serve the needs of the community, but it would nonetheless be a far cry from Socialism as we have known it.

There is a strange irony here. When Socialism was in its early history it was concerned *solely* with taking over capitalism and transforming business methods. The discussion of capitalism was central to its thinking. Now that Socialism is in its dotage it would never dream of intervening in the industrial or business process, since *capitalism* has become not merely a non-discussion topic but a taboo word in left of centre circles. When, therefore, the left moan about all the abuses of what we describe as Rentier capitalism, they have only themselves to blame for their own ignorance and disdain.

Left wing activists (within all levels of organised politics) are completely out of their depth as soon as they discuss the problems of the financial-industrial sector. What, then, is the answer, for state intervention *is* necessary in transforming and monitoring business in the future? The only answer is that those who are sufficiently knowledgeable in financial-industrial matters should be politically empowered in ensuring a smooth and successful transition – providing, of course, they are working within the framework for a Social Capitalist society. In this way we shall see the "old enemies" of Socialism achieving the purposes of the latter which they could not accomplish themselves.

12 – Contrasting attitudes of Experts and Ill-informed to problem-solving

The new politics which is called for – which the world needs for its survival – eschews the vested interests of particular sectors of the population. The new politics in the world of the great middle-middle majority, needs to be so disinterested in its purpose, as to appeal to the reason and commonsense of thinking men and women everywhere, irrespective of their standing in the community. It must be a politics which works on the principle of one nation one world. Never before has there been a greater consensus in the non-American world on what constitutes right and wrong in the field of social life. This is the great opportunity and source for optimism in the future.

Those to the left of centre, whenever they are gathered for discussion, have always tended to argue that correcting the ills of the world is a simple matter. They have usually tended to view the problems of the world as self-evident and free of complication. But in this they have been entirely wrong. The superficial appearance of things rarely reveals their underlying reality, i.e. the causes of why things are as they are, and the attitudes and arguments necessary in effecting desirable change. Advanced industrial economies comprise highly complex organisations, and if *real good* is to be achieved, it is necessary to call on the experience and knowledge of those who are best qualified in relevant spheres of knowledge.

When change is called for, those who are *less* qualified to affect it, usually evoke a confrontational situation. This is because, through their own ignorance, they are working in the dark, and have no alternative but to make a big noise in attracting attention to the cause. We now live in an age when massive change is called for in the near future, and the greater the change or the problems to be faced, then the greater is the prospect for confrontation and its destructive outcome. But when change is called for, those *most* qualified to affect it, always adopt, on the contrary, a technological or constructive approach to the situation. This is because they use their existing knowledge and skills in a problem-solving capacity, without the need for raising issues to a morally emotive level.

Whilst the less qualified tend to raise the moral tone of issues, often in lieu of practical solutions, the more qualified concentrate on the cool activity of applying reason to the objective resolution of problems. For all these reasons it is increasingly urgent to draw greater numbers of the highly-educated into the activity of politics, and to discourage the lesser qualified from participating in political life. This may seem to suggest an anti-democratic attitude, but the truth needs to be faced, that the cultured and highly educated in *all* spheres of knowledge, are repulsed by the apparent superficiality, pomposity, stupidity, oddity, and doubtful mental balance, of those who are drawn into active politics. This applies equally to activists across the political spectrum.

Tories portrayed at Conference gatherings or garden parties, are no less caricatures of what they supposedly represent, than are Labour supporters at their Conferences or demonstrations, and the general public (including the best amongst them) recoil at what they see. Over the years I have attempted to draw friends and acquaintances into making a political commitment, but always the response has been along the lines of, "I agree with the underlying aims of the party, but I'm just not prepared to associate with those kind of people."

And the expression of such dismissive gestures are not infrequent events. They reflect attitudes universally held. And neither should they be condemned as prejudice or bias. They reflect the feelings and disdain of ordinary people, dismayed at what they perceive as the exaggerated or distorted view of those without a balanced perspective of the world. Most truths are to be found at the centre of the Golden Mean, at either end of which only falsehood exists. And, sadly, the left/right perspective of political life encourages – if not makes inevitable – a polarisation of problems and their solution. This pattern of democratic life may not always contribute towards *extremism*, but it goes some way in that direction, and the public dislikes what it sees.

13 – Launching the politics of tomorrow

This is yet another reason why in the age of the great middle-middle majority, there is decreasing support for party political systems, as presently structured throughout the industrialised world. Thinking well-balanced men and women are just no longer prepared to support a divisive politics which twists all issues to suit discredited ideologies no longer able to advance human progress. The majority demand something better to engage their political sympathies. And that better can only come from the disinterested politics of promoting the welfare of all humanity within an organised framework for justice and equity.

The call for a new politics, centred around social capitalism in confronting the might of America's Rentier capitalist ideology, is a huge but necessary challenge in upholding democratic values and systems which have evolved over a 400-year period; in addition to the even greater task of saving the planet. This would entail the implementation of ten Great Projects. The first project in throwing down the gauntlet to the world tyrant, would therefore be the formulation in depth of the theory and practice of Social Capitalist philosophy. This is a purely intellectual activity, drawing on the knowledge-base of the past whilst also utilising available research. The purpose of this exercise is to arouse the imagination and inspire thinking people with an entirely new political perspective.

Such intellectual activity, although it should be encouraged worldwide, must concentrate its efforts within Europe and the Far East Tigers, for it is in these advanced industrialised territories, where its truth will sooner strike a chord and attract most support. Whilst books and pamphlets on Social Capitalism will initially be of most interest within academic circles, every effort should be made to spread the message to the general public in drawing up a new political elite.

The second project would be to establish a voluntary organisation based within nation states under the umbrella of an international office; and the third project would be to engage the cooperation of existing parliamentary bodies, possibly with the idea of their absorption. At that stage *Freedom From America International* would have emerged from the status of a voluntary association in entering the realm of practical politics.

The fourth project would entail cooperation between states with regard to reversing the inroads of American capitalism; legislation for appropriating or breaking up American corporations and conglomerates; measures for reviving the Productive capitalism[30] and social democratic consensus undermined by US penetration in the 1980s and 1990s; the re-establishment of credit industrial investment banks and the enabling of commercially viable deficit financing; and laws

---

[30] It would be useful here to differentiate between the terms Social and Productive capitalism. The latter is a technical term describing the mainline system of capitalism designed to supersede the exploitative pattern of the Rentier economy. I have presented the theory and practice of Productive capitalism in four major works cited earlier in this book. However, this does not preclude other forms of capitalism which may be examined and comfortably implemented alongside Productive capitalism; and for this purpose, the broader term Social capitalism is used to embrace all theories worthy of investigation in challenging the ills of Rentier capitalism.

Various Cooperative systems clearly fall under the heading of Social capitalism, and other leading practical theories which are being advanced in political and academic circles, are *Capital Partnership*, as promoted by my friend, Chris Cook (an ex-City financier and stockbroker); the *Altruistic Economics* of Robin Upton (who is applying his principles in Bangladesh where he currently lives); the *Binary Economics* of Rodney Shakespeare (who has successfully aroused interest in his theories in academic circles in Indonesia); and finally, mention must be made of the superb work of the Rev. Canon Peter Challen in London, in research, in promoting the research of others, and in acting as an invaluable contact link as the Chairman of the Christian Council for Monetary Justice, and the London Global Table which meets weekly throughout the year.

facilitating the more equal cultural participation of nation states internationally.

The fifth project would constitute philanthropic policies by the non-American advanced industrialised world, i.e. Europe, Russia, the Far East Tigers, and China, for the relief of suffering in the Third world, comprising advisory banking services for the internal capitalisation of states; assistance with regard to agriculture and irrigation; the building of hospitals and the training of medical staff; and the establishment of universities and the supply of teaching personnel, with particular emphasis on the social sciences, systems of democracy, and social ethics.

14 – Confronting climate change with clean energy

The subsequent projects will entail the reversal of climate change, and planetary measures for re-establishing a balanced eco-system and a safe environment for all forms of life. Such projects could only be successfully achieved on a scale so large, and through the participation of all nation states by so close a cooperation, that the attempt could not be envisaged without the assistance of a unified and worldwide political ideology. And this is the reason why freedom from America must be accomplished before any such projects may be embarked upon.

That is, the politico-economic direction of America, both ideologically and in practice, veers so far in a contrary direction, that the rest of the world cannot afford to wait for a change of thinking. Of course, an environmentally healthy planet cannot be achieved without the eventual cooperation of the USA, but the non-American world must meanwhile organise and progress according to its own best intentions until such time as America is brought aboard. And the latter cannot be achieved until she has transformed her Rentier economy into a system of Social or Productive capitalism.

If the world is to be turned into a *Global village*, in terms of amity, understanding and cooperation, this calls for educational and cultural exchange schemes on a scale never before undertaken in history. Whilst on the one hand all nation states will be urged to safeguard their economic and cultural integrity (particularly with regard to maintaining living standards, full employment, and restricting immigration); on the other hand, international friendship and inter-marriage between peoples of different nationality and cultures would be increasingly encouraged, especially amongst those with higher levels of education.

Such encouragement could be made through the inducement of giving employment priority to mixed marriage couples in the higher echelons of politics, the civil service, industry and the professions. Such proposals are not made out of a light-headed sentiment to promote international friendship but as a serious strategy for increasing the bond between *separate* peoples and strengthening the practicalities of successful cooperation. The ultimate purpose of such a strategy should be to reduce grounds for international conflict and make the occurrence of war a decreasing possibility.

The sixth project would entail the Great Renewable Energy plan, and in utilising the latest technology in transporting electricity, huge photovoltaic solar panels would be erected across the Sahara from Morocco to the Western desert in Egypt to supply clean power for Europe and Russia west of the Urals. In Saudi Arabia similar Electrical Power farms would be erected for supplying power to western Siberia. These electrical plants would earn considerable revenues for Morocco, Algeria, Libya, Egypt, and Saudi Arabia, and under the auspices of Social capitalism would be made to benefit ordinary people, and so not end up in the pockets of a small shareholding elite, as would usually have occurred in an earlier epoch under American domination.

15 – Desalination, Afforestation and Hydrogen power

But the greater benefits of solar power to these peoples across northern Africa and Arabia, would be derived through the seventh project, entailing irrigation for agriculture and the afforestation of vast areas of potentially fertile desert. Huge canals and pipelines would be constructed from the Mediterranean to hundreds of miles inland. Along the canals would be saltmarsh vegetation, rushes, mangrove trees and shrubs, in creating a more humid environment; but more significantly, at intervals along the canals and pipelines, desalination plants would be constructed, utilising the technology of multistage-flash distillation systems.

At the present time more than 8,000,000 cubic metres (or 2,112,000,000 gallons) of fresh water is produced daily by several thousand desalination plants throughout the world, and in embarking on this new project, an attempt would be made to increase this daily production ten-fold within a 15-year period. Desalination projects are always costly, and require power, and this would be available through the latest solar technology. This would entail the first step in bringing prosperity to the most impoverished on our globe.

The eighth project would comprise an afforestation programme across the Sahara and in Saudi Arabia, under the leading management of Finnish timber corporations. This is because Finnish companies have already successfully completed afforestation projects in the United Arab Emirates, where their personnel have won and maintained the trust and love of Arab rulers. Already by the mid-1980s, it was claimed that the climate had become noticeably milder, with a more than average annual rainfall, due to the afforestation of the desert – the road from Abu Dhabi to the oasis town of Al Ain being lined with palms for most of the route, each tree being watered by miles of punctured hose. At the same time afforestation programmes would be embarked upon in many other parts of the world, as varied from the Highlands of Scotland to the remote mountains of north western China, not only to effect climate change but as a renewable source for manufactured products.

The ninth project would entail sponsoring research into an alternative to fossil or oil-based fuel for vehicles, with particular emphasis on the possibilities of clean hydrogen power. As soon as innovation had been sufficiently developed, governments would liaise with the automotive industry in speeding the change of manufacturing processes and attending to possible difficulties with regard to the re-deployment of labour. Although the great international oil companies claim widely to be in the forefront of research and innovation with regard to exploring the possibilities of self-sustainable or cleaner energy sources, there remains the suspicion that this in fact is not the case, and that the vested interests of producers, such as the Gulf States, Nigeria, Venezuela, USA, etc., is on the contrary to hold back scientific invention. It is for this reason that the relevant departments of a reconstituted UN (as described below), should motivate academic bodies throughout the world to produce a practical and commercially viable outcome.

16 – A National Planetary Service

The tenth and last project would be to establish a National Planetary Service (NPS) within all nation states, operating closely on an international level. This would entail a universal call-up of those between 18 and 25 of both sexes, for a 2-year period of service. The NPS would be organised on a military style basis, but with a gentler mode of discipline, and its purpose would be concerned solely with environmental projects.

In the front rank of tasks would be those attending to national disasters: earthquakes, floods, the consequences of volcanic irruptions, and storms. In the second rank of tasks would be those concerned with erecting photovoltaic solar panels on the roofs of buildings, constructing wave, tidal and wind generating electricity generating plants; building geothermal systems wherever the geological conditions are appropriate; manufacturing renewable biomass fuels; and utilising nuclear fusion which in the future has the potential of producing vast amount of perpetual energy at a low cost and with minimal waste. In the third rank of tasks would be those involved in building dykes along seashores and river banks against rising sea levels.

The funds for raising the force would be levied in the same way that national armies are maintained, but the highest Command at Staff level, would be international and maintained at the UN HQ. The HQ of the National Planetary Service would be responsible for establishing salary levels according to rank and skills, amending conditions of service from time to time, and authorising the organisation of emergency appeals and longer term projects. Foreign service, i.e. the transfer of Regiments or Battalions to different parts of the world would be necessary in ensuring speed, efficiency, and ease of operations to be undertaken.

Whilst each national NPS would in size or numbers be proportional to its population, its value as an international agency could only be measured in proportion to its service to the total needs of the planet. That is, it could not look upon itself in any intelligible way as an autonomous body in promoting national interests. Hence its culture and ideals would essentially be international in promoting the *practical functions* of global friendship.

The armies of different NPS bodies would differ considerably in skill levels and operational practice according to the culture of their peoples. For example, whilst considerable numbers of Indonesian or Nigerian labourers may be sent to build up the dykes of the North Sea coastline, and the river banks of Europe; smaller numbers of Belgian or Austrian biologists may be sent to the first two countries, to explore the possibilities for improving agricultural methods and irrigation. Whilst British scientists and their Companies of assistants may be sent to Xinjiang province to investigate the means for the afforestation of the Taklikmakon desert; Chinese and Dutch engineers and their battalions may be sent to the mouths of the Ganges in Bangladesh to embark on projects for transforming flood plains into an agricultural paradise.

It is because the costs of environmental problems are beyond the means of even the wealthiest states, and because all such problems cross national boundaries and are global in their implications, that a Central World Bank of the NPS, should be established for funding both emergency crises and longer term projects. The urgency and scale of climate change alone is such that international financial arrangements must be made for supporting the NPS which are agreeable to all nation states, and do not give rise to unresolvable differences.

17 – America incapable of meeting the funding needs of the environment

Although those projects cited above calling for major engineering construction, or scientific innovation, would be organised by relatively autonomous international bodies in ensuring their success and effective funding, it would be necessary that they are brought under the umbrella of a reconstituted United Nations. It can already be seen by anyone conversant with international funding or banking institutions, as they exist today under the shadow of American power, that it would be quite impossible to raise sufficient funds in reversing the environmental degeneration of our planet through utilising the channels of Rentier capitalism. This is because the latter would be unable, firstly, to arrange lending terms of sufficient length; and secondly, to pay out dividends with an acceptably high return in satisfying the markets as we know them; and thirdly, to raise the required capital in the first place.

These are all reasons for pressing a campaign against the economic system of America, which today is dangerously seen as the economic system of the world. Until such time as the economic domination of America is thrown aside, there is simply no point in embarking on any measures in attempting to save our planet. Only through the flexibility of Social (or Productive) capitalism is it possible to set about the essential task of reversing climate change and the other ills upsetting the natural balance of life. The role of the United Nations should be to negotiate with the governments, national banks, and other financial institutions, of all nation states, in ensuring that sufficient capital is raised.

But the primary role of a reconstituted UN would be to achieve what humankind has yearned for for millennia, and is only now within practicable reach. That is, the achievement of permanent world peace! With the prospect that global conflict means mutual self-destruction; and with the understanding for the first time in history that the priority of government is the promotion of majority interests within a free, just, and equitable society; and in the light that these things should be made to fit the psychological needs of humanity and social ethics, humankind should now be sufficiently equipped to avoid the possibility of war.

Now in the 21st century we are sufficiently equipped in knowledge and science to lead rational lives and to promote the cause of rational government. This does not mean we can rest in complacency, for the securing of eternal peace as a political practicality, can only be achieved through the organisation and intelligence of the best amongst the leadership of those of goodwill amongst the peoples of the world. And it is such people who should be brought as delegates to a reconstituted United Nations.

18 – Reconstituting the United Nations

The need to reconstitute the UN has now become an urgent necessity, and its present failure to meet the expected standards and ideals of the peoples of the world cannot be allowed to be a cause for cynicism, since its intended function is irreplaceable. But a fresh start needs to be made, and in such a way that it strikes the imagination and inspires the hope of us all.

The United Nations should be re-located from America (where little love would be lost) to the banks of Lake Chad in Niger, within close distance of Nigeria Cameroon and Chad. The purpose of transferring the UN to the heart of the African continent is motivated by the fact that in the latter are to be found the most intractable socio-economic problems amongst peoples in our strife-torn world today. A new and magnificent city would be built on the banks of the lake to house the international community, and in reflecting a spirit of peace and permanence on its inhabitants, it would be constructed in a pleasing classical style with colonnades, atria, cool fountains, symmetrically laid out gardens, well-proportioned stone-built apartment blocks, and conference centres worthy of the great cities of the past.

A reconstituted UN must be a unified international body with real authority and power, and for this purpose its ideals should coalesce around the principles of Social capitalism and the ideas of justice and equity which this embodies. The weakness of the present body has stemmed from the vagueness of its written intentions, its exposure to faction, and finally, its exploitation by the vested interests of American capital, particularly as influenced through the International Monetary Fund and the notorious guidelines and outcome of the associated Bretton Woods institutions.

A unified UN with real power can only hope to be effective if it is modelled, as if in preparation, for taking on the eventual role of world government. Its existing structure, which may be seen as circular, with the Secretary-General at its centre, may be suitable as a talking shop for some 159 states of equal standing, but as a basis for decision-making it invites faction and Byzantine intrigue. It should instead have a more hierarchical structure with a President and Vice-President subject to re-election by secret ballot every five years, by the 800 or so delegates of the General Assembly, assuming that each nation state sends five delegates.

Answerable to the President would be a Cabinet of fifteen ministers, heading such departments as: Health, Education, Peace-Keeping, Poverty Relief, Agriculture, Finance, Industrial Funding, International Borrowing (it is necessary that the previous two should operate as separate ministries under Finance), Trade Controls (for adjusting and overseeing the import duties of nation states), Disaster Relief, Human Rights, Environment, Science & Innovation, National Adjudication Disputes, and Women's Rights. Another fifteen departments outside the Cabinet might include: Employment Rights, Child Welfare, Religious Organisations, Trade Unions, Refugee Relief, International Law, Police, etc.

No attempt has been made in prioritising the above ministries, since their priority, or placement or displacement within the Cabinet, would change from time to time according to circumstances. Again, each of the above ministers would be subject to re-election by secret ballot every five years by the delegates of the General Assembly. The purpose of such a Cabinet system would be to give a *face* to an organisation which hitherto has been faceless. That is, each minister would seek to raise his international profile directly with the ordinary public through formulating the distinctive philosophy of his department and its policy intentions within the accepted framework of Social capitalism, so that the citizen of Austria, for example, might have as clear a picture of the personality and policies of the United Nations Minister for Health, as that of the equivalent minister in his own country.

This would go far in making the UN a more accountable and democratic organisation in the eyes of the world. The authority of the President and Cabinet would consequently transform the mindset of the delegates to the General Assembly. The delegates would themselves be elected directly by the public from amongst the states(wo)men and leading politicians of their respective countries. They would stand for election, not according to their party interests or allegiances, but according to their presentation of a particular programme for world government, and so in this way, through a competitive electoral process, the United Nations would become a genuinely democratic body.

Of the five delegates from each nation state, only two would carry a mandate from their government. The other three would at *all* times be held to represent the higher moral interest of their electorates in regard to the interests of peace, all humanity, and the environment. Nonetheless, all five would seek to work in harmony, and cooperate and settle differences before addressing the Assembly on any controversial issue.

When the delegates then gather at the General Assembly, it will inevitably be in a very different spirit from the sessions of the unreformed body.

They will gather not as a body of conspirators carrying the secret agendas of their governments, each prepared to stab the other in the back, but as informed men and women (most with specialities in some sphere of public service, government, or business) inspired by the idealism to create a better world. The existing departments of the United Nations would become answerable to the various ministries; and when the General Assembly was not in full session, its members would be busily employed as officers in fulfilling a variety of functions within the organisation.

A reconstituted United Nations on the banks of Lake Chad must call upon the expertise of the most skilled and learned advisers available, and to ensure that an ambience of scholarship and authority pervades the organisation at its start, the first initiative must be taken by the advanced industrial countries of Europe, China, Russia, the Far East Tigers, and the South Pacific states of Australia and New Zealand.

If these states, through close cooperation together, were unable to prevail upon the UN for reconstituting the organisation, then they might embark upon the option of establishing a separate reformed UN, whilst nonetheless retaining amicable and workable relationships with the older body. These industrialised states, however, would gradually withdraw their funding from the various subsidiary organisations of the older body as they developed the reconstituted and improved services from the banks of Lake Chad.

*****

CHAPTER 6

DE-FUSING THE CAUSES OF TERROR

"The deregulation, liberalisation and privatisation of economy and society is the dogmatic neo-liberal response to settling the problems of the modern world. But it is not the most effective way forward in the reconciliation of economic success with social justice."

Robert Taylor, *Sweden's New Social Democratic Model*, Compass, 2005, p. 5.

1 – Political injustice gave rise to terrorism

There are several causes of conflict in the world today which threaten to draw our planet into a maelstrom of chaos and destruction, and since their endemic severity tends to be exacerbated by the blundering of American diplomacy, or military might, it is necessary to discuss their possible resolution by a non-American world.

A world free from America must seize the opportunity to promote a greater understanding between peoples in crisis, and the greatest political threat today in fracturing relations with a significant cultural sector of the earth's population is the latent conflict with the Islamic world. A political conflict has been created and allowed to fester out of all proportion due to the crass stupidity of American power politics. America's declaration of the War against Terror, was not only absurd in concept and unprecedented in the history of warfare as properly defined, but culminated in the irrational response of hitting out blindly at windmills mistaken for giants.

George W. Bush's war against Iraq was a desperate attempt to seek out a revenge victim at any cost. But it was plainly an attack on the wrong target. It also entailed the destruction of one of the only secular states in the Arab world. It was, furthermore, the *only* Arab state with which Osama bin Laden, the originator of the first great act of terror, was in opposition with regard to religion, politics, and the foundations of social life. Despite all the tyranny and atrocities of Saddam Hussein (and the scale of these should not be minimised) he was never a military threat to America or to the Western world. He was, on the contrary, a former ally of America, which supplied him with his one-time weapons of mass destruction of the civilian population.

Saddam Hussein was the leader of the Baath party, a secular pan-Arab Socialist movement, founded through the benign intentions of German advisers, during a period of war, for the modernisation of the Arab world. The Baath party may have degenerated over the decades into an instrument of oppression, but it nonetheless was one of the few organisations in the Middle East which carried the seeds for planting a genuine understanding with the West, and it was this movement which the Americans set out to destroy. In its place, we are seeing the emergence of an ugly theocratic state, the crushing of secularism, the return of superstition and fundamentalism, a posse of quarrelling mullahs jostling for power, and a collapse into anarchy. And this is what the Americans call their gift of democracy!

America's unjustified war against Iraq added fuel to the fundamentalist flame, not only amongst the Arab nations, but throughout the Islamic world. Territories which hitherto had only known peace between Muslims and their neighbours, suddenly encountered unrest, violence, and outrages inflicted on innocent victims. Most noticeably beyond the Arab world, these occurred in southern Thailand (a Buddhist people renowned for their peaceable nature); in the southern Philippines, against the Catholic majority, in the only Christian state in the Orient; and in the eastern peripheral regions of Indonesia against a number of non-Islamic minorities. The Bali bombings of Jamaah Islamiyah under the inspiration of the imprisoned cleric Abu Bakar Bashir have become especially notorious.

But the crimes of America in the Middle East date long before this period. What brought about the original terrorist attack in the first place? What caused the Arabs to turn in on themselves and revert to a life-denying and politically self-destructive fundamentalism? All these things came about through the tribulations of injustice, and the usual clumsy machinations of

American policy which bring impoverishment and suffering in their wake.

The festering sore which never heals and now poisons the entire body of the Arab world is the tragic question of Israel and the Palestinians. Never in the history of the modern world was there ever such an example of injustice, such an outrage against common sense and ordinary decency, committed with such insouciance, as legislation for the cool expulsion of the Palestinian people from their homeland of a thousand years. They were dispossessed and cleared from their lands as if ridding an infestation of rats, to make way for those with no legal rights of settlement whatsoever.

2 – Liberal values are the key to inter-racial concord

The attitude of America, and shamefully, of some other governments too, was that here was a primitive oriental people – of *Untermenschen* – who could be expediently overridden in serving the higher needs of not merely a superior Western people, but of God's own chosen race. The truth, of course, was that the Palestinians were not a people who would be overridden. They would prolong their fight for justice, if necessary, until the day of Judgement and by any means within the realm of possibility. Furthermore, it needs to be added that the Palestinians have always been amongst the most educated, forward-looking, and energetic of Arab peoples.

Their ease in accepting the benefits of Western civilisation is in part accountable to the mixture of their racial and cultural origins, for these often fair-haired and blue-eyed people can trace an ancestry to the Greeks of the Byzantine empire, and to the Crusaders from Germany, England, Italy, Sweden, and a dozen other territories of Western Europe. It should also be borne in mind that not all Arabs are Islamic, for there are many ancient Christian Arab communities. For all these reasons, the non-American world – and especially Europeans, should regard the Palestinians as their blood brothers and sisters.

America has long been the military ally of Israel, supplying her with weaponry to crush her indignant neighbours on all fronts. During all the negotiations over decades into which America has entered on both sides, in gestures to resolve the on-going conflict, she has never addressed the real underlying problem, and that is why a secure peace has never emerged. American negotiators have always been prepared to discuss the petty peripheral issues of the Israeli-Palestinian conflict but never the central issue of justice or serious compensation. Europeans, on the other hand (intent on burying the shame of earlier attitudes), together with most of the non-American world, are now sympathetic to the Arab cause in recognising an injustice which must be undone.

How, then, can this intractable problem be finally resolved? Israel cannot be wished away. It has been brought into being and it must surely stay. No propositions for the dismantling of Israel could ever be put forward for serious discussion. Only two alternatives remain, and it is probable that both should be undertaken together. The first is in regard to compensation in terms of land, housing, and money; and the second is in regard to reconstituting the Israeli state, enlarging its territory to satisfy the Jewish population, but creating a liberal democracy so that Jews and Arabs may live in peace as equal partners.

Under such an arrangement, two languages would be legally recognised, and displayed in street signs, shops and offices, and all government notices would be dual-language, and legislation would be passed for ensuring equality of opportunity in all spheres of life. Whilst the state would be strictly secular in its administration, it would officially recognise Judaism and Islam as the two state religions on an equal par – but as a liberal democracy, it would allow the practice of all other religions and sects.

Whilst Jews and Arabs would have their own language schools, newspapers, and publications, mixed schools would also be established, and intermarriage between the two Semitic races would be encouraged, through granting employment priority and promotion to the partners of mixed marriages and their offspring.

Advisers from Finland and Belgium (both countries with two substantial language groups) would be sent to monitor the successful transition of Israel into a dual-cultural state. The government would need to legislate for an average 50/50 population mix between the two races, so that neither would appear to overrun or dominate the other in any functional spheres of employment.

3 – Religious bigotry is always self-destructive

The question of sufficient compensation for the dispossessed Palestinians, and the return to their homeland – if not to the actual plots from which they were originally evicted – needs to be carefully considered. It would not be acceptable if Israel, or a greatly extended Israeli state, was to be overrun by a poor or unemployed Arab population. Palestinian compensation would need to be raised through a tax on Middle East oil production, and the return to the homeland would be gradual, according to the grant of visas, and return to completed housing projects, farmsteads, and the prospects of immediate employment. The energy and intelligence of the Palestinian people should make such a transference of the population to Israel a smooth and successful operation.

How practical are such schemes? The question should rather be asked, How essential have they become,? for there are no other thinkable alternatives. A strategy of mutual and everlasting attrition could be maintained, but it would be self-destructive and only succeed in sustaining a living hatred. A very dear Chinese friend once expressed her exasperation and bewilderment at the confrontational stupidity of Jews and Arabs, comparing them unfavourably with the Chinese and the impossibility of such futile strife within the framework of a Confucian culture. The Chinese, she insisted, avoid confronting those with whom they differ, and are sensitive to the fact that those with whom they *could* fall into enmity, must never be allowed to lose face. I reminded her that Semites in the blinding light of the desert could only perceive objects or ideas in terms of black or white, and that there was no room for shades of grey in their culture, and that this was reflected in the literature of both Jews and Arabs.

Such a view of the world made for the abrasiveness of forthright opinion, an irritability with perceived wrong-doing and a tendency towards self-righteousness; and this explosive mix led inescapably to a quarrelsome temperament. Those with fixed notions find compromise difficult, and those who are arrogant in their own "virtue" will never lessen their pride. Moreover, when such characteristics are expressed through the conviction of a dogmatic faith, then the social or political consequences are exacerbated ten-fold. The only hope in our own time for the resolution of the Israeli-Palestinian conflict therefore lies in the pressure which may be brought to bear by the millions of liberal-minded Jews in the industrialised West.

The Jews of Europe may indeed be happy to sponsor a reconstituted Jewish state where all races may live in harmony – not just Jews and Arabs – but the political Zionism of American Jewry, with its foolish bias and subjectivity, is unlikely to give way to the demands of justice. If the one-sided sympathies of American power are allowed to continue in the future as they have done in the past, their blundering diplomacy may lead to the destruction of Israel and another diaspora of her people.

4 – Worldwide Jewry must resist the mischief of American diplomacy

This is the reason why Israelis must resist both American influence and that of her Orthodox religious leaders who drove their people to political extremes and catastrophe on numberless occasions during the ancient history of their people. A comparison may be made between the stubbornness of Israel's Orthodox religious political leaders today and those who dominated public opinion in the hundred or so years of the Roman occupation leading up the diaspora of 70 AD. The Roman administration was always accommodating to the religious beliefs and practices of different cultures, but petty quibbling over the representation of images, the erection of signs and monuments, and the symbolic deification of the Emperor, who presided over what continued as the republican and electoral institutions of Rome, was eventually to bring a costly disaster on the Jews of Palestine.[31]

The Roman administration was never anti-Semitic, and attempted to satisfy the more extreme demands of religious leaders with little success, and if there had been a greater spirit of toleration amongst the Orthodox, much bloodshed and strife could have been avoided in Palestine in the years leading up to the diaspora. It should also be borne in mind, that during this period, large communities of liberal-minded Jews were already happily settled in Rome[32] and Alexandria, and other cities throughout the empire. All this would seem to demonstrate that in the ancient world, as in the modern, the Jewish problem of Israel should be perceived as a local or territorial issue and not an issue of worldwide Jewry. It is only the intervention of the American state, in conjunction with the mischievous desires of her fundamentalist Christian churches for expanding a Zionist Israel, which threatens to stoke the flames of an already inflammatory situation.

There therefore remains the fearful premonition that modern Israel is not averse to following the disastrous example of her ancient past. Surely it needs to be reiterated that in the world of the third millennium, there is no alternative to the generosity of liberal values for peace and prosperity for the sake of *all* humanity. Any nation state in the contemporary world, when confronted by the threat of conflict, must surely look to the higher priority of all humankind as against the pursuit of more narrow interests which through the accident of events may draw the world into a maelstrom. That is, although the Israeli-Palestinian conflict may be perceived as local from a purely Jewish perspective, its political implications are nonetheless threatening to worldwide peace, and that is why we have devoted so much space to the question in this book.

---

[31] See especially chapters xv and xvi of Gibbon's *History of the Decline & Fall of the Roman Empire*, on the politically troublesome nature of the Jews.
[32] It has recently been estimated that 400 synagogues flourished in Rome during the time of the Antonines.

5 – Why the Islamic and Western civilisations are incompatible

There is another issue which needs to be considered with regard to a long-term peace settlement in the Middle East and the security of peoples worldwide. This concerns questions arising from the civilisation of Islam, particularly in the Arab world, Iran, Pakistan, and India. Over the past decade, much has been discussed about the alleged incompatibility of Islam with the demands of Western civilisation – and the peoples of the Far East are included in this latter category. Much is spoken about the clash of civilisations, and the coming conflict – and such a conflict must never be allowed to occur on our planet.

But how can the tension be released, and how can the foundations be laid for preparing a meeting of minds? American leaders pass over the question with blithe indifference by notionally acknowledging Islam as a good in itself, as it *is* after all a religion, and hence desirable, since agnosticism in the American view is an unacceptable alternative. In Europe, a real attempt is made to accommodate an understanding of Islam by ordinary people, through evening courses, books, etc., but it is doubtful if this one-sided effort can ever hope to change the worsening pattern of political events.

If the question is to be addressed with sincerity, the fact needs to be acknowledged with candour that there exists an underlying incompatibility between Islam as it presently exists in the Arab world, and the wider world of Western technology. It is a divide which somehow *must* be bridged for ensuring global peace and security. There was an era, some 800 years ago, when Arabic civilisation in the Western half of the world dominated all the spheres of learning, science, and literature, whilst Europe meanwhile lingered in a state of gothic ignorance and barbarism. Now the situation has almost been reversed.

The underlying problem is that whilst Western science, civilisation, and progress, can neither be maintained nor advanced without the existence of a liberal free-thinking mindset, and all the consequences which this entails; Islamic civilisation, within the constraints of its present framework, cannot survive without upholding its set of totalitarian rules for the conduct of life in which so many of its beliefs are centred. The religious Islamic life is complete and exclusive within a defined mode of thinking and acting, within which all happiness and contentment is supposedly to be found.

The objection which Arabic-Islamic peoples find in Western civilisation is the perception of its anarchic freedom and immorality – all of which is ugly, frightening, and unacceptable on any terms. For example, almost all the conditions of Western social and domestic life are perceived as shocking and immoral: the social mixing of men and women; men and women dining at the same table; implications of dietary prohibitions; dress codes; modes of ablutions; most forms of public entertainment (irrespective of whether both men and women may be present); lone unaccompanied women leaving the house for any reason (e.g. household shopping), etc.

It is surprising, but nonetheless true, that those freedoms adopted by the West during the past hundred years, e.g., the enfranchisement of women and the extension of their legal rights; common law relationships; sexual incontinence between men and women; contraception; the legalisation of homosexuality, etc., are condemned with hardly less rigour than those cited in the previous paragraph. It should be noted, however, that the above and other freedoms are not achieved through the causation alone of a struggle for extending rights, but more significantly, through the pressures of technological change and its impact on society, which enforce the need for such rights in facilitating smoother interaction and greater flexibility in promoting progress.

Hence it is technology and changing social structures which dictate morality and not vice versa, and it is this which Islamic peoples fail to understand and refuse to acknowledge. They fail to understand it since their cultural world remains within the theoretical framework of a static society; and they refuse to acknowledge it since they confuse morality with the principles of ethics. That is, whilst morality is no more than accepted custom on right and wrong as perceived at a particular point in historical time, ethics is concerned with the underlying principles (or science) of right and wrong as objectively understood, and as applied to humanity and the cosmos irrespective of a time factor.

6 – The political secularism of the non-American world must confront the political religiosity of the USA

Whilst America and the Arabic-Islamic world, through the separate fundamentalisms of their religiosity, are obsessed with the false consciousness of morality; the enlightened peoples of the rest of the planet are increasingly concerned with profound ethical issues as a means for resolving the troubles of our time. It is because of this that the American political system is unable to begin addressing the problem of Islamic civilisation: i.e. it is too absorbed within the subjectivity of its self-righteousness and religious view of existence.

It therefore falls to the secularism of Europe and the Far East Tigers to address this problem. There is only one viable course to follow. The peoples of the Islamic world must organise a Conference to discuss how the Islamic faith and its way of life may be made more acceptable to thinking peoples beyond the embrace of their own religion. The purpose of such a Conference would not necessarily be to change the principles or practices of the faith, but only to present an intellectual construct as a possible hypothesis for the future.

For example, it would be inconceivable to the peoples of the West and the Far East, that they should live in a world where around mid-day and early evening, the religious police enter shops and public places, waving camel sticks in the faces of customers and shopkeepers, ordering them to leave and lock up their premises and go to payer; or that the police should arrest men and women in the streets or parks for being improperly attired; or arrest couples of the opposite sex seen holding hands; or forbid men and women from being employed in the same workplace; or close all night clubs, cinemas, and theatres as places of immorality; or forbid the sale or consumption of alcohol.

To suggest that the above prohibitions are even thinkable may sound absurd, but it should be borne in mind that there are not an inconsiderable number of Islamic clerics now living in the West, who actually advocate and expect that such legislation should eventually be passed by the parliaments of the industrialised world. Moreover, in their innermost hearts, they believe they are residing in hateful societies of the utmost wickedness and degradation, and like the Marxist revolutionaries of an earlier epoch, they only live for the day for overthrowing the established order.

The notion that the *Shariah* law should be introduced into the societies of the industrialised West is made all the more a possibility in the eyes of these Imams and Mullahs through the emergence and hardening of exclusively ethnic communities and no-go areas of Asians, and those of African descent, throughout Britain, France and Germany. These religious leaders, who already have their Islamic parliaments and control committees, feel they have rights, which cannot be denied, in regard to governing their communities according to their own laws. In September 2005, Trevor Phillips, Chairman of the Council for Racial Equality, produced an authoritative report demonstrating how Britain was becoming an increasingly divisive society. This was not due to the discrimination of the white population, but rather due to the Islamic cultures' choice of exclusion, and resistance against the very idea of integration. This would make for an unhealthy and explosive situation in any society.

7 – An Islamic Conference to promote international understanding

Only those belonging to the Islamic faith would participate in such a Conference, but observers from all faiths and none should be encouraged to witness the debates and conclusions drawn. The Conference should, firstly, be representative of Islamic states, the delegates being proportionate to the Islamic populations of those states; and secondly, and most importantly, delegates should be represented from those other states where their religion is in a minority: e.g., India, Britain, Germany, France, etc. As Saudi Arabia remains the guardian of the most holy places, the Conference should be held in Riyadh under the auspices and chairmanship of appointed liberal-minded princes of the Saudi family, and no time limit should be put on the length of the Conference or on the remit of relevant topics for discussion.

The Conference should open by defining the essence of the Islamic faith, i.e. the indivisibility of God, the underlining universality and equality of humanity, and a world and society governed for the promotion of peace. It may be argued that the Islamic conception of an impersonal God as an abstraction of goodness, places the religion on a higher evolutionary plain than its Abrahamic predecessors of Judaism and Christianity. This would at once raise the morale and hope of delegates towards the prospect of a successful outcome. The resort to Western sources in supporting Islam should be encouraged, e.g. through quoting Bayle, Voltaire, and Gibbon, and especially Carlyle, who evoked Mohammed as his Hero in the sphere of religious life. All this would add credibility in the eyes of Europeans.

If the Conference was to be held in the light of Social capitalism, as an emerging political ideology, this would be especially encouraging to the participants of such an assembly. This is because the purpose of such a Conference would be to break down the intellectual and psychological divide between the Islamic and non-Islamic worlds, and from a certain aspect, Social capitalism could be conceived as *designed* to satisfy the ethical demands of Islamic commerce. That is, although Social capitalism does not call for the abolition of the charging of interest (indeed, it regards it as essential for the capitalisation of major projects), its core philosophy is that excessive interest, or *usury* as understood in its modern sense, is not merely a social evil through the macro-economic outcome of polarising wealth, or rich and poor, but that it is ultimately self-destructive in undermining commercially viable productivity, or production for use.

The idea of benign Social or Productive capitalism confronting malign Unsocial or Rentier capitalism, goes far in satisfying the theological ideas of Islam on ethically acceptable modes of business. Hence a non-American world of Social capitalism would at once de-fuse much anger and resentment against the West. It would also entail a significant step in disarming Terrorism as a technique for warfare in the fight for justice. Furthermore, the holistic approach of Social capitalism in embracing the needs and interests of all humanity, as opposed to representing the vested interests of specific groups or classes, is again in correlation with the Islamic view of bringing religion, ethics, and politics within a unified framework.

8 – Women and freedom in Islamic societies

As soon as the proposed Conference had considered the positive and substantive values of Islam, it would then turn to discussing those controversial issues, or aspects of Islam which are unacceptable to the industrialised non-Islamic world. The first of these concerns the status of women. It is unacceptable throughout the modern industrialised world that there should not be equally shared rights between men and women in most spheres of life and work, and these include: freedom of movement; privacy and autonomy within the private sphere; free association with the opposite sex in the spheres of domestic and work life, and chosen fields of leisure and social activity; freedom of choice in regard to dress; freedom to drive a vehicle; freedom from the fear of Honour killings; freedom from the practice of female circumcision (a form of mutilation which should be forbidden by law) preventing the pleasure of sex; freedom from arranged or forced marriage (each of which cannot be properly differentiated from the other) and, equality with regard to the weight of evidence given in a court of law.

It should be borne in mind that we are here concerned with the rights that such a Conference should recognise for non-Islamic peoples, and not necessarily for those of their own faith, and so the debate would clearly circulate around theoretical possibilities and not the practical implementation of new proposals. It would anyway be impossible to change the pattern of Islamic life solely through legislating for the ideas expressed above, for the outcome could be social anarchy and the breakdown of natural inhibition and moral constraint – conditions intolerable in any society.

Arabs have a false perception of Westerners as living in a kind of social chaos, and sexual promiscuity, since the former are so restricted by laws and customs that they cannot imagine the maintenance of propriety or decency without them. The reality, of course, is that Westerners live in very self-disciplined societies, where the rules of conduct are no less numerous and hardly less strict than those to be found on the Arabian peninsula. The difference, however, is that whilst Islamic rules of conduct are made specific through written codes, those of the more sophisticated West tend to be hidden within the unwritten rules of historical tradition.

It is often asserted by female propagandists of the Islamic faith that they are indeed free: free through the protection of their own menfolk from the dangers and evils of the outside world; free to own and manage property as widows or sole inheritors, and free to safeguard their modesty from the prying eyes of men through wearing the burkah or some other veiled garment. But the opinion of non-Islamic womanhood is not moved by these or other arguments. A forced reliance on the protection of others may be interpreted as patronising or demeaning; or an attempt to reduce adults to a childhood status; or a subtle attempt at domination for a host of different reasons. The three brothers with whom I worked in Saudi Arabia, for example, rarely allowed their women to go on shopping expeditions. They projected themselves as good domesticated husbands, who shared the household tasks, and whilst one brother shopped for meat, another shopped for fruit and vegetables, whilst the third shopped for toiletries, cosmetics, tampons, etc.

When I once suggested to one of the brothers, that perhaps their womenfolk might prefer to choose their own toiletry products, as we drove along a highway, he pointed out of the window to a group of women fighting in the street behind a bus. "That's what happens when you let women out alone," he exclaimed. On Saudi buses seating is only provided for men. In a separate entrance at the back of the bus there is a small sealed-off standing room only compartment, and when this becomes filled to a crush, there is sometimes a quarrelsome struggle to mount the vehicle. "Our family believe in sparing our womenfolk from that kind of stress and humiliation," concluded my friend. So much, then, for the freedom of Islamic women, and we have not touched on the widespread custom of Honour killings, and the torture and mutilation of women alleged to be guilty of a roving eye. In these respects Islamic civilisation stands accused by an affrighted world that could never stand silent in the shadow of such injustice.

9 – The question of polygamy

The greatest objection of the industrialised world to Islamic civilisation is usually the toleration given to the widespread practice of polygamy. I have discussed this issue with Arabs throughout the Middle East, and whilst the less affluent have tended to dismiss the topic with a laugh, exclaiming that, "more than one wife *always* leads to trouble," and calls for never-ending diplomacy in mending relationships; the wealthy have always defended polygamy on a variety of spurious grounds, viz: that they are offering protection and fulfilment to women who would otherwise remain unmarried; that it offers legally-endorsed sexual satisfaction to women who might otherwise fall into immorality; that men are by nature not monogamous, and therefore need more than one sexual partner; that all wives are treated fairly and equally, as required by religious precept (although the practicality of this is doubtful); and that it is the will of God that men should be allowed up to four wives.

It may be true that men are by nature not monogamous, but then to a slightly lesser extent, the same may be said of women. The sexual instinct is no respecter of law or custom in any established society – except perhaps, amongst certain island peoples of the South Pacific – and that is why all societies, except the most oppressively puritanical, have been obliged to make some kind of arrangements for illicit relationships. It is because of a worldwide hypocrisy on sexual matters, that they arouse the strongest feelings, and are so closely identified with the concept of morality that the two are confused as one and the same. If the demands of psychology are taken as an objective basis for resolving the conflict of sexual relationships in a just and egalitarian society, then the law is bound to recognise equal rights between men and women, and then legislate from that basis. And the outcome in most civilisations, and most of the contemporary world, is the call for monogamous relationships.

How could the problem of Islamic polygamy, therefore, be resolved to the satisfaction of the West? In equalising opportunity, it might be suggested that polyandry be legalised, so creating marital relationships as once existed in Celtic Britain, but this would be an absurd and unacceptable solution. A call for the abolition of the many Turkish-style harems throughout the Middle East would be strongly resented, in the same way that you cannot remove a hind from the herd of a dominant stag. And besides, the closure of harems would lead to unnecessary suffering, social ostracism, and impoverishment of great number of wives and concubines. An answer to the issue is perhaps best approached by looking at the evolving freedom of women in Western societies over the past few centuries, and then taking a lesson from that.

Whilst the great Sheikhs, Emirs, and Kings of the region could hardly be prevailed upon to compromise their status by surrendering their nominal rights of ownership over wives and concubines, extending the rights of women within their domain, might be a first step in transforming relationships from one of suppression to that of freedom. That is, if the walled and closed palaces of the region could be opened to the light of day, and their communities converted into Royal or noble courts, as centres of entertainment and government in an aura of culture and magnificence, it might be a first step towards a greater equality between the sexes.

Wives and concubines would be freed from the stifling environment and monotonous existence of entertaining one another, to becoming mistresses in an open society where they might entertain or become advisers to courtiers and visitors from the outside world. Such ruling palaces might model their courts on those of 16th and 17th century France, which with their polite formality and rules of conduct smoothed the way for the social acceptance of illicit relationships. As such courts offered a happy example to most the royal houses and nobility of Europe, in facilitating civilised and free relationships between the sexes, there is no reason why they should not also be offered as a paradigm to the princes of the Islamic world of the 21st century, as a staging post in the evolution towards a more democratic society.

Although certain aspects of the French courts may be distasteful or offensive, there are two consequences of their influence, trickling down to all sectors of society, which needs to be noted. Firstly, their bearing on civilising manners and relationships between the sexes; and secondly and of equal significance, their bearing on democratising relationships and freeing women from social and legal constraints under which they had formerly existed. Hence by the start of the 18th century it had become unacceptable in the higher echelons of society for men to tyrannise over women without attracting ridicule or contumely. When the future George I of England divorced his wife, Sophia Dorothea, in 1694, following a liaison with a handsome adventurer (who was assassinated for his attentions), and then imprisoned her for the remaining 32 years of her life, he was therefore justly regarded in many circles as a barbarian and tyrant in committing an outrage against a royal princess.

Such reforms tentatively outlined above would not therefore be proposed as an end in themselves, but merely as a means towards the eventual abolition of polygamy and concubinage in a better world a generation ahead. Whilst certain privileges, unacceptable in the West, would be retained for the present generation of the greater Sheikhs, Emirs, and Kings, of the Middle East (and others in the Far East), their descendants, through education and contact with the industrialised world, would culturally assimilate the idea of monogamous marriage.

Immense social changes are entailed in moving from a polygamous to a monogamous society, and it should be remembered by the West, that it is only through the benefits of oil wealth that these old traditions have been maintained and expanded on a larger scale than hitherto. Polygamy is regarded with abhorrence by most the peoples of the world, not only as grossly immoral in itself in satisfying the sexual greed of men, but as a gross injustice against the rights of women. It is these cultural questions which need to be brought to the attention of Islamic religious leaders.

It therefore falls as a kind of moral obligation on the West to initiate ideas for establishing monogamous societies in the region, since the West was/is responsible indirectly for financing the harems of the Arab princes through the course of commerce. And such changes cannot be effected through single-step legislation, but only through a staging process of historical progression as suggested above.

10 – Reforming *Shariah* law

Another wide-ranging topic for debate by such a Conference would be the need to reform *Shariah* law, which through the pressures of fundamentalism, is now being established in territories where it never existed before in modern times. The horrendous penalties of the *Shariah* code, which are defended on the grounds they stem from Divine law, are regarded with universal repugnance by the non-Islamic world as barbaric and out of all proportion to the offences committed. Any legal system should allow for the reform and the re-integration of its offenders into society, but how can this be achieved successfully when men and women have their limbs lopped off?

Every legal system should be sufficiently flexible to allow for the expression of moderation or forgiveness, but how is this possible in the face of horrific penalties? At the commencement of every legal document in the Islamic world, reference is made to the "All-merciful God," but if the *Shariah* law is taken as the word of the All-mighty, such a phrase cannot but strike a hollow note of hypocrisy, evoking a wry smile of incredulity. And the eight offices giving rise to the death penalty,[33] of either beheading of public stoning, convey the impression of a harsh and unforgiving society dominated by feelings of vengeance.

But the greater injustice of *Shariah* law lies not in its penalties but in its procedures. Whilst the penalties are publicly inflicted in a great ceremonial of religiosity after Friday prayers, so that the crowds might be instilled with horror at the idea of sin, the examination and trial of alleged offenders are conducted in camera. Rational or factual evidence is often treated as an irrelevance within the *Shariah* system, whilst the use of forensic evidence is practically unknown. Hence the use of confession and self-accusation are relied upon in securing conviction – being types of evidence repudiated as invalid by every legal system in the civilised world.

In Islamic societies the normal procedure is for an arrested person, prior to questioning or even a criminal charge, is flogging or torture with an electric baton, before a written statement is placed before the accused for signature. In *Shariah* courts dealing with either civil or criminal cases, evidence is weighed or accepted not primarily according to its intrinsic worth, but according to the status of the witnesses called. Hence the word of a Moslem is taken against that of a non-Moslem, and the word of a man is taken against that of a woman.

A medieval religiosity pervades the *Shariah* court in its mode and style of practice, which seems to separate it by a thousand years from the modernity of the 21st century. The *Qadis* presiding over Islamic courts have the qualities of priests rather than those of lawyers, and although they may be learned in the Koran and Hadiths and the codes of the *Shariah*, as mystics and religious enthusiasts, they are unfitted to the task of weighing solid evidence. In the eyes of the industrialised world, the entire body of *Shariah* law, together with its procedures, needs to be overhauled and then reformed, as otherwise a permanent barrier

---

[33] These are, adultery, sodomy, apostasy, bestiality, robbery with violence, trading in drugs, rape and murder.

exists between an understanding on fairness and equity in dividing Islamic civilisation from the rest of the planet.

Another circumstance arising from dissatisfaction with Islamic law in the West, is that any allegedly illegal immigrant from the Middle East or North Africa, only has to claim that he (or she) will be tortured, or otherwise ill-used, if returned to his own country, to ensure the rights of permanent residence. No Western country is so lacking in humanity as to refuse the rights of permanent residence, if the alternative means facing the horrors of Islamic penalties. But if the legal systems and procedures of Islamic law were reformed to match the standards of the West, then much prompter action might be taken in deporting those who were unwelcome on our shores.

11 – A hierarchical Islamic church for sanity and stability

In helping to bring into fruition the above proposals in uniting the Islamic and non-Islamic worlds, the Conference called for this purpose, should look to re-organising the Islamic church as a great body of global intellectual learning. It is probable that all the troubles besetting the Islamic faith in dividing its followers from the rest of humanity, stem from the ignorance of their Imams and Mullahs who are learned in the teaching of sacred texts, but are unqualified in every other department of life, and particularly in the knowledge of cultures beyond their own experience. They are unfortunately placed in the unhappy situation of thriving in a closed intellectual environment which disdains everything beyond its limits, and this repudiation of the outside world sets up ignorance as a kind of virtue.

An argument may be presented that an autonomous priestly class of often self-selected equals, and only answerable to God, presents an unreliable basis for a stable and evolving church. Although its leaders (of usually equal status) may be inspired or fanatical in their conviction and faith, a jealous and vigilant eye tends to ensure that all are bound in equality through *opposition to change*. Hence prejudice and conservatism strengthens such a church through suspicion of any who attempt to rise above the rest in terms of hated innovation.

It is this psychology of ignorance, operating as a mechanism throughout the priesthood, which blocks the possibility of progress or change. Whilst on the one hand the autonomy of the Islamic religious leader (for he should not correctly be referred to as a priest) assures him a freedom from the authority of officially appointed superiors, and the freedom to enthuse in his faith and preach as he chooses within a given framework; on the other hand, he is not subject to the correction or moderating influence of those more qualified who might when necessary, hold him in check. All this contributes to both the solidarity and insularity of a church which is made to view the outside world with aversion and enmity.

If the Islamic church is therefore to meet the intellectual standards of the industrialised world, and engage in the language of its thinking, it might well be to its advantage to establish a hierarchy of officially appointed priests, modelled possibly, on the Roman Catholic or Anglican churches. Such a church would need to be established under the auspices of a university, and its benefits to the Islamic faith would be considerable: firstly, in founding an authoritative and stable body in meeting the needs of the modern world; and secondly, as an effective launching pad in disseminating the faith amongst peoples in the non-Islamic world.

At the head of the Islamic church would be a personable and popular priest with a liberal education, able and happy to mix with ease amongst notabilities and peoples of any culture or background, and of any religion or none. He should be clean-shaven in attracting worldwide credibility; be at sufficient ease with the media in gaining desirable and widespread publicity; and as with the Dalai Lama or the Pope, should have a kindly disposition in winning the respect and love of many millions not adhering to the faith.

At a lower level in the hierarchy would be university-educated scholars, not only learned in the theology of their religion, but in history, psychology, the arts, and other humanities. These priests would be responsible for designing a liberal educational system throughout the Islamic world, with particular emphasis on science and engineering, in raising their peoples to an equal level with those in Europe or the Far East.

A third level of priests would be responsible for church discipline over the fourth level who would work in mosques at parish level. A more detailed Calendar than had existed hitherto would be prepared for prayers, sermons, and special rituals, and these would be designed to occupy the time and concentration of parish priests, in diverting them from heretical or mischievous activities. All priests would be obliged to undergo a 3-year training in comparative theology before being permitted to preach or officiate in any way in the life or services of the mosque, and the role of lay persons as prayer leaders, or other functionaries in conducting any aspect of religious life, should be abolished forever.

12 – Dissenting Christian clerics often no less mischievous than those of Islam

It should be pointed out that the need for a structured hierarchy in safeguarding against the emergence of religious demagogues, dangerous bigots, and bloodthirsty clerics in calling upon their congregations to throw away their lives in suicide bombings, is not aimed only at the Islamic faith. Christian dissenting sects, reliant on the fervour of their followers, are just as mischievous, and the rabble-rousing hate-merchants amongst the extremist Presbyterian clergy of Northern Ireland, for example, are no less evil in their intentions than any Imam to be found in Egypt, Iran, Saudi Arabia, or Iraq.

The dissenting cleric from a remote Ulster village is no less ignorant, uncompromising, repugnant and narrow in his religious outlook than the average prayer leader to be found on any grimy back street in the Middle East. A broad education, on the other hand, and employment within the structure of a disciplined hierarchy, and the human contact of correction and competition, ensures a level-headed attitude and an attachment to reality.

In conclusion, on this topic, we must return to the essence of Islamic theology, which is to be found in the indivisibility of an impersonal deity. This gives Islam an enormous advantage over the other great religions in developing a modern theological-philosophical concept of God which is denied the other faiths – or at least, makes it difficult for them. Christianity with its twisted theology of three-Gods-in-one; its mixture of pagan beliefs; and its pre-historical rituals in eating the body and drinking the blood of the deity (described as formulas of magic by anthropologists), place theologians in a difficult situation in describing the nature of God intelligibly or convincingly. In the last resort, for want of intellectual power – and despite the generosity of their outlook – they are usually obliged to fall back on faith or superstition.

Islam, on the other hand, is fortunately free of these intellectual hoops which have to be jumped through. If it was to update its theology (as the Christian churches have, for the most part, succeeded in doing over the past few centuries) and sought to give a rationally symbolic interpretation to the mix of myth and history, as opposed to a literal reading of events and texts, it would quickly find the path to attracting many millions to the faith throughout the West. The way would be open to utilising the thought of Spinoza and Hegel in defining the nature of God, or the thinking of A.N. Whitehead and Julian Huxley, in giving a deeper meaning to religion for the peoples of the third millennium.

This is an opportunity for Islam – for worldwide peace – in spreading its eternal message. But it is only possible through accepting wholeheartedly the liberal values of modernity. And this is because the advancement of our complex, multicultural, and technological world is only made possible by the adoption of such values. Arab-Islamic peoples may be fearful at the appearance of what they see as the materialistic West, but their anxiety is misplaced, for humankind is everywhere and at all times endowed with a religious instinct. But religions need to evolve in the same way as material progress. And the religions of the future will be different from those of the past. They will be inspired by the certainties of rational thought, and the eternal verities in satisfying the psychological needs of humankind. Will Islam take up the challenge and flourish, or will it retreat into itself and reject the benefits of modernity?

13 – A dialogue with Islam is an imperative for world peace

These are all issues for the great Conference designed to unite the Islamic and non-Islamic worlds, and to rid the peoples of the planet from the fear of Terror and further conflict. If the discussion or negotiation of such a Conference in Riyadh was to end in deadlock, or break down in acrimony, the session could be closed and re-located in Jakarta, capital of the country peopled by the Moslem majority of the world.

The Malays of Indonesia and the adjoining peninsula on the southern tip of the Asian landmass are a gentle but far-sighted people, keen on modernising their countries, and enjoying the cultural and material benefits of Western civilisation. Whilst they are fully committed to the Islamic faith, they are also free of those puritanical inhibitions and marks of severity which mar the religiosity of the Arabs – especially of the dominating Wahabi sect.

Psychologically, it is probable that the Malays are better placed to accept and promote a modernised and more liberal form of Islam. Furthermore, their institutes of learning, in both Malaysia and Indonesia, are more geared to innovation and research, and their peoples exert a greater energy in both work and leisure. Trisakti University in Jakarta has already won an international reputation in hosting conferences to discuss the issues of Islamic business and lending, and how these may be correlated with Western practice. It would certainly be preferable if such a Conference, as we have outlined, could be held in Saudi Arabia, since in the view of the Islamic world majority, this would add greater credibility to its outcome and success, but if this is not possible, then the option has to be taken for the second choice.

The assertion may be made that it is presumptuous to pontificate on the need of reforming a culture, other than one's own, irrespective of whether it be secular or religious. The attempt at such a task some twenty or thirty years ago would have been taken as an outrage in treading on the rights and feelings of autonomous people, or as an unwarranted attempt at imperialist-style interference. But today in the 21st century we are faced, in regard to Islam, with a quite exceptional situation. The world is faced with a powder keg, and by a cultural-political situation which cannot be handled by the ordinary means of diplomacy.

The rest of the world can no longer be expected to accept Islam on its own terms. If it does so it is merely waiting for the time-bomb of war to explode. This is because there are no remaining grounds for the industrialised West to discuss the basis for a secure and permanent peace. Security for the world and peace for Islam can only be realised through a process of *equalising the chances* for both conflicting world outlooks, and this can only be attained through liberalising Islamic culture in opening up the channels for intellectual dialogue and the exchange of constructive views.

It is this which not merely justifies but makes imperative the broad proposals we have outlined above. It should be borne in mind that politically explosive situations with regard to Islamic civilisation pertain in the Middle East with regard to the Israeli-Palestinian crisis; in Iraq with regard to a three-way conflict between Shias, Sunnis and Kurds; in central Asia with regard to Chechnya, and elsewhere with regard to oil politics; and worldwide, with regard to fundamentalism's war of Terror against the industrialised economies.

14 – De-fusing the future social crisis in India

But the threat of new terror comes from other quarters, also, and most disturbingly, from Hindu nationalism in India. The Indians have long been amongst the most civilised peoples on earth with regard to the toleration of difference (if one excepts the Independence racial crisis during the formation of Pakistan and the division of Kashmir), and their peoples have generally been kindly and rational during national disasters, or in difficult crowd situations. Nonetheless, approaching problems of huge proportions, confront the peoples of the Indian sub-continent.

A casual visitor from an industrialised economy would quickly conclude that here was a country with all the conditions for a successful Marxist revolution. He or she would be appalled by the poverty and suffering contrasted by the display of conspicuous wealth. He would be shocked by social injustice on a scale he could never have imagined, and would marvel at the endurance of humanity in resisting the urge to rebellion. India boasts she represents the world's largest or most populous democracy, but the Westerner would look askance at such an assertion, exclaiming, "Then what has this democracy achieved for the downtrodden masses?" Until the present time it is "the opium of religion" which has kept the Indian masses in their place, and fatalism and acceptance of suffering, and an Asiatic determinism, making for an apolitical view of existence.

Meanwhile, Indian party politics is inscrutable and Byzantine. But such a situation is unlikely to last for much longer. The newly-emerging and powerful middle class are foregoing the values of the past, not out of choice but out of necessity, in meeting the demands of technology, consumerism, a cruel competition of life, and the changing sociology of work, and these things will eventually bring them into conflict with the subordinate masses. Such a conflict is unlikely to repeat the revolutionary patterns of Europe, as anticipated by Old Socialism in the West, but is more likely to express itself in a growing Hindu fundamentalism, when a once peaceful people are again transformed into the *Thugs* of an earlier epoch. Such bloodshed may be confined to India, but its economic repercussions would not, and for this reason we must address the possibility of such a catastrophe.

It needs to be understood that the Indian mind is often an extraordinary mixture of science and superstition. Graduates with a technological background will give accounts of wondrous and miraculous happenings as if they were based on fact; and assert as reality stories which defy the laws of dynamics and physical existence. On the other hand they have a good reasoning sense, and a love for speculation, and metaphysical discussion. The great weakness of their political intellectual life, which could eventually lead their country into a time of troubles, is the lack of an underlying rationale for unifying all sectors of society within the state in promoting justice and equity.

There is the need to create a dynamic and truly *political state* out of the mishmash of vested interests and variety of conflicting beliefs which currently comprise the so-called political system. What energising force can hope to transform the mindset of India on the questions of government, justice, and the basis for an ethical secular society? It is not suggested that Britain should interfere in Indian matters – our influence in the spheres of administration and law have been widespread and are generally benign – but it is proposed that the German authorities establish schools of Hegelian philosophy throughout all the states of India.

Such schools would aim to implant new ideas on the nature of the state and its relationship with the individual; identify the unity of opposites: spirit and nature, universal and particular, and the ideal and real; point out the synthesis in which all the partial and contradictory philosophies of Hegel's predecessors are alike contained and transcended; and generally give meaning to the concepts of truth, life, and existence which give a greater credibility than alternative modes of thinking.

The primary underlying purpose of disseminating Hegelian philosophy would be to create a rational mindset making the political acceptance of freedom, justice, and egalitarianism an imperative practicality. It is the all-embracing and constructive nature of Hegel's philosophy which gives value to his system as a universal guide to life and existence, and in pushing out adherence to earlier beliefs. The schools would be maintained to a high standard by German academics, and their attraction to students of the political and social sciences, religion, philosophy, and other disciplines, would be found in the quality of their European-based degrees.

Politically liberal patterns of thought will be essential in achieving a stable and peaceful world, and although toleration of difference amongst varying cultures may be found in many parts of the world, this is not in itself sufficient in ensuring lasting concord. The breakdown of harmony and a slide into conflict and bloodshed, in such places as Yugoslavia and central Asia, demonstrates this fact. There is a distinction, therefore, between simple toleration which may be friable, and a political liberalism which establishes toleration on a firmer basis. Western Europe is the heartland of such liberal values which consciously promotes a universal fraternity, and because of this, she has a duty to spread her message of peace across the world through practical means.

Her best way of undertaking such a task would be for such countries as Britain, France, Germany, the Benelux countries, and the Scandinavian states, to train their minorities or Guest Workers in relevant aspects of culture and political science, before returning them as an exclusive elite to their ancestral homelands (or places of origin) to take up leading positions in government, teaching, and the other professions. These policies would naturally be coordinated through the will and cooperation of the recipient states, which would assess demographic conditions before indicating the numbers of doctors, dentists, economists, scientists, lecturers, etc., they would like to receive from the donor countries. Such a strategy in advancing the life-chances and industrialisation of the African peoples would be of particular value in helping to create a more prosperous, egalitarian and secure world.

15 – The non-American world will carry the torch of progress

If the good of humanity is to be assured for the longer term, this can only be achieved through changing the way people think. This is in sharp contrast to the practice of violence as resorted to by America whenever she perceives the possibility of turmoil or conflict in any part of the world. It should be no surprise, therefore, that over the past forty years, on almost every occasion, her military intervention (for whatever reason) has either led to the failure of her original strategy, or to the reduction of territories to a more pitiful state than they were in before.

The accidental or unintentional infliction of misery, war damage, or death, or the consequential establishment of horrific dictatorships with their injustice and cruelty, is no lesser an evil than if they were not accidental or unintentional. It has never been implied in this book that America or her people are by nature vicious or sadistic, even though her political system has given rise to acts which are vicious and sadistic. The unforgettable sin and crime of America against the world is her blundering ignorance and stupidity, and most of all, her false political philosophy which is responsible for these ills. It is bad thinking which leads to bad actions.

It therefore falls to the non-American world to achieve good for the greater part of humankind. And this is not to be achieved through war, since it is counter-productive through the resentment it arouses; and neither is it to be achieved wholly through diplomacy, since the guile it entails evokes suspicion and misunderstanding; and so good is predominantly achieved through visionary planning, and the enlightened approach of refusing to accept current thinking and accepted wisdom in those places wherever strife and misery raises its ugly head. Utilising imagination through relevant knowledge of crisis situations is the key to problem-solving, and it is this which has been so lacking in America's use of her power. Europe and the Far East must take over the torch for the peace and progress of our planet, and for the protection of the environment.

But before the peoples of the non-American world can organise to confront the threat of the once mighty power, they must first look to avoiding the dangers of fifth-columnists in their midst. In all nations, there are still those in politics, in finance, in corporate business, and even in academia, prepared to take the thirty pieces of silver in selling truth for falsehood; and in doing so, to knowingly betray their own countries in exchange for the privilege of standing in the light of the giant's glamour. Such perfidy is easily committed when the temptations are so great, but it is the weak, the superficial and the ill-informed, who most easily fall into the tempter's web.

16 – The underlying unity between Europe and the Far East

There are those in public life who are well known for the misjudgements they have made, and justifiably, they are exposed to obloquy and scorn. Sometimes regret may be their sufficient punishment, but there are others who work in darker corners, usually in business or as economic advisers for the vested interests of others, and these need to be confronted and exposed to the light of day with open argument and candour. A political campaign, fought on many fronts, for freedom from America, must be sufficiently effective in convincing the majority that the expression of pro-American views, or worse still, actually promoting American interests, is not merely self-destructive but even treasonable.

This is because, as shown in earlier chapters, America is contemptuous towards the feelings and needs of all peoples and nation states, and to her allies no less than to her foes. This is partly because she is now a debtor nation, struggling to balance her books, but it is predominantly because of her aversion to what is foreign and unknown. The spirit of *true* or lasting friendship is unknown to her political system, for she is only capable of appreciating relationships of dominance and subordination. No trust can be placed in her treaties or agreements, for they are only made for the financial exploitation of smaller states. It is for these reasons she must be projected as the pariah of the world.

There are seemingly political leaders in this country (and elsewhere) who are oblivious to the hindrances of the Rentier economy, and of the immense damage rendered by the influence of American power. It is no coincidence that Britain has a higher criminality rate and more of her population behind bars than any other European country. It is no coincidence that there has been a polarisation between poverty and wealth since 1997, and that Britain today has the worst educational system of any advanced industrial country excepting only for America.

We are no longer even capable of producing doctors, dentists, scientists, or other highly skilled professionals from amongst our own population, whilst examination standards amongst all levels of study are dumbed-down to meet collapsing expectations of success. Meanwhile the standards of broadcasting (in both radio and TV) are sacrificed to a debasing populism which threatens to turn our people into hopeless morons.

The political protagonists of the American way boast that our economy has never been "stronger," but they are blind to the catastrophe which lies ahead. Have they never assessed the inevitable implications of a banking system which intentionally relies on increasing levels of personal debt; or an economy which by default promotes de-industrialisation and the unaffordability of housing for the younger generation; or the reasons why the Labour government is allowing the NHS and other supporting agencies to fall into decline? All these social ills are due *directly* to the subtle American takeover of the economy, and that is why our politicians must be challenged to defend the economic and cultural integrity of our country against its greatest foe.

Despite the arguments in earlier chapters demonstrating the failure of democracy to exert its will through our out-dated representative structures, we are nonetheless obliged, through the demands of realism, to recognise the "As is" situation. This means we must continue to work through existing party systems. The campaign for anti-Americanism must therefore be pursued through parliamentary groups across the entire spectrum of left/right politics, as well as through non-governmental organisations and other functional bodies. Trade associations and manufacturing federations throughout the world should be especially active in raising their defences.

Although small or medium-sized independent American enterprises should not be subject to the above discrimination – indeed, they should be allowed an equal right to the comparable business of any other country – it is the corporations with their huge financial power which need to be confronted with an uncompromising will. There is clearly a sharp distinction between the ordinary trading company, only intent on the exchange of goods, and the corporation intent on taking over national economies. The consistent purpose of this book has been the promotion of justice and fairness for nation states, and this cannot be maintained unless there is a level playing field for all.

If sometime in the future America was to experience a cultural-political revolution in her attitude to the world; and if she was to transform her financial-industrial institutions from a malign power into a beneficent force for the majority of humankind; and if she was to promote democracy, justice, and equity as political realities, I would gladly take up my pen in promoting the cause of *All power to America*. It is not what America *is* but what America is to *become*, which will finally matter in deciding the destiny of our planet. Hence the hope for America's future is the hope for us all.

If we turn to the non-American world, and especially to the many states of Europe and the Far East Tigers and China, we encounter nation states and peoples who strive for peace, harmony, and understanding. They accept the reality they are thrown together in the great melting pot of our global village, and they are curious about the cultures and customs of one another, and they value the qualities of love and international friendship above all else, since they recognise the necessity of interdependence. They have a common understanding that each nation state must preserve its economic and cultural integrity against the intrusive meddling of either federations or the threat of international corporate power.

They also realise there are nations on our planet which feel afflicted in a world of incompatible cultures, and others which are poor and helpless to raise their peoples out of famine and degradation, and in this book, we have outlined projects for resolving such difficulties and crises. Europe and the Far East, with their benevolence, culture and ancient civilisations, forged through the suffering of history, are ideally placed to help the misguided, the confused and the oppressed, through the enlightenment of education, and their better understanding of social ethics in making the world safer for justice and equity.

And above all, these enlightened nations with their combined economic strength, supported by a population of billions, are destined eventually through mere absence of mind, if not by design, to prevail over what is today perceived as the "mighty" power. And that latter will eventually witness a victory for the greater happiness, harmony, justice, and equity of her people, and when that day is realised it will mark the ultimate unity of humankind towards a long age of peace and progress.

******

APPENDIX A

Draft proposals for an association to be known as, *Freedom From America International*:-

PREAMBLE DEFINING THE PARAMETERS OF FREEDOM FROM AMERICA INTERNATIONAL (FFAI)

A non-partisan appeal transcending the interests of nationality, race, class or religion, in the struggle of peoples to maintain their rights of political, economic and cultural integrity

The major ills of the modern world are accountable to the malign power of America in the spheres of international finance, politics, and a short-attention-span-deficiency culture undermining civilisation throughout the world

The politico-economic power of America is directly and uniquely responsible on a global scale for –

1. Destroying freedom and democracy howsoever these may be defined as sociological realities;
2. Exacerbating poverty, famine and political oppression;
3. Promoting a financial-industrial system which through its internal nature polarises wealth between rich and poor;
4. Raping the environment whilst obliviously failing to participate in desirable measures for conserving the living needs of the planet;
5. Advancing a deceptive socio-political ideal based solely on the concept of growth which sacrifices the need for community cooperation to satisfy egoistic desires; and,
6. Encouraging a superficial culture which subordinates the civilising process of thought to the blind motivations of instinct.

To counter these social ills an appeal is presented to oppose undesirable American power in all its manifestations, cultural as well as economic –

1. As the most effective means in achieving world justice and equity in countries both poor and affluent;
2. As the only means for drawing attention to newly emerging political realities of concern to all humanity;
3. As the best means for securing global cooperation for the practical resolution of the world's most intractable problems;
4. To build successfully the foundations for friendship and cooperation between peoples and their governments;
5. To create a political vision and set of principles to unify peoples across the globe in the struggle for a better future; and,
6. To help renew the United Nations as an inspired, enlarged, and more powerful organisation for freedom, justice, and equity, for all peoples as equal citizens of the world.

The virtue of democracy is not simply in that it empowers people, but that it –

1. Attacks and breaks down ossified institutions whose once-benign purposes have become oppressive; and,
2. Advances progress on the wave of new ideas through the benefit of the social sciences.

It is these purposes which underpin the function of this appeal in calling upon the goodwill and active support of kings and presidents; of rich and poor; and political parties in all their diversity committed to the better governance of independent states.

This appeal welcomes in the spirit of friendship the active support of all American citizens of goodwill who support the underlying socio-economic principles described below for these alone comprise the sole end-purpose of this initiative.

The Strategic purpose of the FFAI –

1 – World peace and stability can only be secured by a united front against every aspect of American foreign policy and financial intervention in territories beyond her borders.

2 – The defensive onslaught against America must be non-party political in seeking to attract all nations irrespective of their political systems or ideology.

3 – Aggressive or first-strike war, as now pursued by America, must be outlawed as unacceptable under any circumstances, and this conviction underlies the primary justification for the existence and strategy of the FFAI.

4 – As the lone superpower, dominating politically and financially the affairs of the world, America must be identified as the Number One Enemy, and all lawful means taken in the struggle to diminish her might in the cause of peace and justice.

5 – Each nation state, or national HQ of the FFAI, may adopt or re-formulate its own defensive strategy against America, providing only that it acts in a spirit of co-operation with the International HQ, and acts within the law of its own territory, and in disseminating information, maintains objective standards of verifiable truth.

6 – It is held that no strategy alternative to the reduction of American power and influence can hope to bring peace, stability and prosperity to the peoples of the world for the longer term.

7 – The aims and strategy of *Freedom From America International* should be seen and interpreted purely as a means for achieving justice and equity amongst the peoples of the world, and in no way as ends in themselves.

APPENDIX B

Draft proposals for a manifesto for *Freedom From America International*

The Manifesto of Freedom From America International
or
The Sixty-five Theses Against The World Bully

I - The worldwide threat to cultural autonomy –

1 – The omnipotence of America in dominating the nations of the world has become so extensive and so malign that nothing less than a direct challenge to that power will suffice in the necessary struggle for recovering regional autonomy and in establishing international co-operation amongst peoples with equal rights.

2 – As such a movement must appeal to all peoples, irrespective of their system of government or stage of economic development, a campaign must be launched which puts emphasis on the undesirable characteristics of the American world outlook, for the perception of her people as stupid, insensitive, foolish and philistine, and well-deserving the ridicule they attract, is universal and invariable throughout the four corners of the globe.

3 – Meanwhile, many territories have specific grievous perceptions of America according to their experience of exploitation, oppression, or war, as victims of the world bully, and the FFAI should support all groups and nations in the promotion of those perceptions and the solutions to issues which are called for from that.

4 – Whilst the FFAI should not be seen as a movement which is against the American individual *per se*, it recognises the collectivity as an evident reality of our time, and hence justifies

the generalisation as a starting point for formulating a defensive counter-attack on behalf of the world community.

5 – America is the one superpower in the world today through the prerogative of her wealth, global currency, corporate power, military might, land mass, and insatiable will to international domination, and it is these forces which must be challenged in upholding the rights, the diversity, the cultures, and the civilisation of the world.

II - A declaration of defiance in defence of civilisation –

1 – The time is long overdue for the peoples of the world to defend their values and culture from the onslaught of American degeneracy and exploitation.

2 – All peoples have the right to defend their cultural, economic, and political integrity, from the threat and actual domination of the world's superpower and bully.

3 – The time has arrived for co-operation and friendship amongst all peoples in a united front against American influence or power in any form or guise.

4 – Any means within the law of states is justified in the struggle for autonomy against the world tyrant and destroyer of substantive cultural values.

5 – Any declaration which compromised the intent of the above four paragraphs would not only weaken the resolve of the campaign to be undertaken but consign it to failure.

III – The horrors of a war programme –

1 – Ex-CIA director, James Woolsey, tipped to play a leading role in the coalition provisional government for Iraq, declared in a speech attacking the leaders of Egypt and Saudi Arabia in Los

Angeles on 3rd April 2003, that America was "on the march" and involved in a "fourth world war."

2 – The irresponsibility of America's war games stems from their age-old ignorance of cultural and geo-political factors, which will lead to the toppling of delicate balances in unstable regions with horrific consequences for the world.

3 – The given rationale for American war aims is always the establishment of democracy and stability, but experience over the past 50 years has witnessed the occurrence of unforeseen circumstances which bring into being tyrannical dictatorships and institutional arrangements far worse than before.

4 – Measures must be taken to ensure that Britain and all other countries resist entanglement in American adventurism entailing illegal or aggressive acts against any nation state for whatever reason.

5 – It has already been demonstrated that undesired American military force and/or the imposition of financial or trading domination leads directly to acts of terrorism, and that the perpetuation of American power on the international scene will lead inevitably to the increase of terrorism worldwide.

IV – The problem of America –

1 – If America represented a form of civilisation higher or better than that of the developed cultures throughout the Western and Eastern hemispheres, she would be partially (but never wholly) justified in exerting some authority as a superpower, but such pre-eminence is missing in every aspect of her domination.

2 – In terms of culture, international understanding, and political morality, she is on the contrary, secondary to any other developed country, and for these reasons, her influence or domination over other nation states is deleterious to the latter,

and therefore all peoples, in promoting their better interests, are called upon to resist the power of America.

3 – The American people exist under the mistaken illusion of their superiority by reason of their seeming modernity and mishmash origins, which they see as global, blind to the fact that their perception is based on a parody of the past and on the grave of a thousand cultures.

4 – America not merely fails to appreciate other cultures through the isolation or philistinism of her people, but is incapable of such understanding or empathy through a consciousness uniquely different from that of any other nation.

5 –This difference stems from the lack of a psychic sense of traditional roots which is instead replaced by an imposed or synthetic value-system failing to reflect the human condition or to fulfil the balanced needs of the individual.

V – The world usurer –

1 – The artificiality, falseness, and hypocrisy of American ideology, or the "American dream," and the wrenching away from the roots of culture, has its consequences in psychosis, the drug culture, and widespread criminality.

2 – As America is deficient in cultural and spiritual values, the vacuum is filled through the need to measure the worth of all things through their reduction to the cash nexus, and the god of marketing or cash value (the Golden Calf) projected as the Supreme Being, never fails to astonish all other peoples throughout the world.

3 – Hence a country without culture cannot be expected to acknowledge those of others, and because of this, it is no coincidence that America is contemptuous of the susceptibilities and specific needs of peoples everywhere.

4 – The financial-industrial system of America reflects a distinctive capitalism which polarises wealth between rich and poor to a degree unknown amongst other systems for the funding of industrial investment.

5 – American lending, funding or investing in foreign territories, whilst adopting the guise of grinning benevolence, is usually ruinous to recipient peoples due to a combination of double-dealing and usury, leading eventually to poverty, famine, bankruptcy and death.

V I - America against democracy –

1 – As the ruling political parties in America are under the control and ownership of the great corporations, the country is in reality a plutocracy and not a democracy, and the criterion for this conclusion is to be found in the impossibility for the nomination and election of representatives without the endorsement of the financial establishment.

2 – The existence of an electoral system in itself has never been accepted as evidence for democratic government, and just as Republican Rome was never judged a democracy because of limitations placed on those eligible to stand for office, so in contemporary America, the de facto impossibility for the election of those representing the poor or downtrodden, or even majorities.

3 – As American government is in no sense democratic through its inability to represent the substantive interests of the majority, so likewise it is incapable of promoting democracy worldwide, as amply demonstrated over the past 50 years through its undermining of democratic movements and governments, and its sponsorship of vicious dictatorships promoting imprisonment, torture, murder, and the denial of basic human rights, both throughout the Americas and South East Asia.

4 – America's negation of moral values and unfitness to play a leading role on the international scene, is made evident through her single-minded pursuit of money profits, and the ruthless sacrifice of both human needs and the national will of peoples, and also the integrity of established systems for self-subsistent economies.

5 – The peoples of the world must rise to the challenge of fighting the usury of the American corporations and American finance, primarily through internal capitalisation; the empowering of extra-legal economies; and the benefits of intermediate technology recognised as an essential staging post in industrial development, all aimed at ensuring the stability and prosperity of existing communities whilst preventing the trauma and needless destruction of established societies.

VII – How America destroys freedom –

1 – The American Rentier capitalist system (denominated Neo-American capitalism by the French economist Michel Albert) not only concentrates on the maximisation of money profits to the detriment of socially desirable productivity, or market share, but accumulates capital into ever fewer hands.

2 – The outcome of this system not only concentrates financial and political power into the hands of a smaller but increasingly wealthy number of individuals and groups, but decreases the number of those who own and control property in both the domestic and business spheres of activity.

3 – Whilst dispossession in the domestic sphere is achieved through the inflation of property values, whereby mortgages may never be re-paid; in the business sphere, two processes occur to disguise an economy of the dispossessed: firstly through the existence of the subsidiary enterprise maintaining its distinctive logo and identity, whilst remaining nonetheless under the absolute financial control of a corporate office; and secondly, through the existence of the franchise entailing the

financial responsibility of a licensee whose hands are tied with regard to every aspect in the management of the concern.

4 – The American capitalist system, together with its global implications, enforces a standardisation of products and services hardly less ubiquitous than in a Stalinist regime, resulting in greatly diminished consumer choice and declining opportunities for innovation or the realisation for inventors' ideas.

5 – Stemming from the above, and the increasing dependence of a people on conformity imposed by the multifarious manifestations of concentrated financial power, is the loss of opportunity, individuality, freedom, and cultural diversity in every realm of life.

VIII – The onslaught on high culture –

1 – The American ideology of false democracy reflects an outlook which is unprecedented in reducing moral, cultural, and spiritual values to the lowest common denominator.

2 – As the American concept of democracy is based on the cash nexus, financial power is upheld as the final arbiter in all disputes and questions of value, and whilst the realisation of democracy remains the unattainable "pioneering" ideal of the majority, it is commonly experienced through the anarchy of economic relations.

3 – The democratic morality of American life gives credence to the ethical idea of the survival of the fittest in both withholding social justice from those encountering misfortune howsoever met, and in denying the claims of equity whenever they clash with the libertarianism of the powerful.

4 – As the application of the cash nexus as a value system leads inevitably to the simplification of concepts, in the sphere of culture, the arts, and modes of living, all forms and ideas are

reduced to the stereotypical and simple, to align with the idea of a false democracy and imposed egalitarianism, and so the outcome of America's world domination is a threat to all forms of high culture wherever it exists.

5 – The sociology of American egalitarianism is like no other on the planet, for in place of attempting to establish justice and equity, it presents instead an artificial substitute of familiarity, intended as the substance of equality, in disguising the ulterior motives of financial exploitation in gaining the trust and support of the naïve and gullible.

IX – The malign intellectual foundations of American life –

1 – Philosophical pragmatism, a movement founded by William James, John Dewey, C.S. Peirce, and others, at the turn of the 19th and 20th centuries, forms the basis of American intellectual life, and its injurious application is manifested in the fields of education, government, and business.

2 – It is a natural psychological product of the American mentality, complementing the needs of a people with little trust in the past, and dependent on direct experience rather than on established knowledge.

3 – Philosophical pragmatism reflects both a cynicism and hypocrisy towards the idea of truth, and is really an anti-philosophy in the sense that it repudiates all constructive systems of philosophy, and hence turns its back on 3,000 years of Western civilisation.

4 – It is inevitably a philosophy with unethical consequences for the reason that it denies the function of abstraction or thought as an instrument for the resolution of issues in favour of the irrational and fascist-like reliance on actions and their consequences as criteria for judgement and decision-making; and it is no surprise that the reduction of all things to the value

of the cash nexus fits comfortably with the outcome of the system.

5 – The ills of philosophical pragmatism, now deeply embedded in all walks of American life, are amply demonstrated through decision-making which is facile rather than wise; superficial rather than permanent; and erratic rather than considered; and in a mentality which revolts against reflection, and is averse to considering the eternal verities of existence.

X – Why war was inevitable –

1 – The Iraqi War, or some other war in another arbitrarily chosen region, was an inevitable occurrence sometime in the near future, due to the internal stresses within the American-financial network.

2 – The American "free market" economy was already in crisis or near collapse, as indicated through the dramatic fall in stock market and pension fund values; the decline of productivity (especially manufacturing); and the retail sales recession, and the government and industrial establishment were placed in a quandary as how to kick-start the economy.

3 – State intervention alone was the rational and practical approach to such a situation, but as such a path was ideologically impossible in a laissez-faire environment, that road was closed in exploring the options.

4 – The ideology of laissez-faire allows for unimpeded state intervention in one sector only: the arms industry, for military hardware is promoted exclusively by the assumed needs of the state, and so the arms industry is evoked as a necessity in kick-starting the economy successfully through its many and various off-shoots throughout the industrial complex.

5 – To the Americans over the past 50 years war has therefore become a necessity in countering cyclical recession, and this

situation is compounded by the fact of America's existing worldwide military bases and the need to feed what has become the addictive habit of a war programme.

XI – On guard against the common criminal –

1 – There are two reasons why America is the most criminally-motivated country on earth: firstly, because of the inherent injustice of her inequitable political system; and secondly, because of the gun culture and the anarchy of social relations, and the intrinsic incapacity, due to nurture and education, of her people to respect law, order, or ordinary restraint, characteristics well demonstrated in both literature and the film.

2 – The world drug culture was initiated by and is maintained by the American criminal fraternity in alliance with American state agencies such as the CIA, as a means for political control and destroying democratic movements judged disadvantageous to American interests.

3 – Furthermore, wherever American bases are established, drug addiction soon follows in its wake amongst the surrounding civilian populace, and people must call upon their governments to stamp out the American drug culture wherever it is found.

4 – In protecting the civilian population from the criminality of American service personnel, the latter should be placed under close surveillance by the police forces of their host countries.

5 – In view of the high criminality rate amongst American people, and their danger to law-abiding populations everywhere, the former should be subjected to stringent visa and special permit regulations in visiting foreign countries, in the same way that America imposes punitive restrictions on all non-nationals wishing to visit her country.

XII – Uniting against the evil empire –

1 – The campaign against America is a worldwide movement, addressing all peoples and nations of goodwill, irrespective of their political systems or ideologies, and therefore diversity must be respected and the message simplified in appealing equally to the sensitivities of all.

2 – Some states, apprehensive of American revanchist tendencies, may wish officially to repudiate the campaign, whilst clandestinely nonetheless giving it their support, and facilities must be made available for all such desired co-operation in the struggle against the evil empire.

3 – Whilst *Freedom From America International* will remain a democratic body with a single endorsed set of aims, working from an international office, the body will operate nationally in a variety of ways on different levels of activity, according to the interests and needs of various territories.

4 – The association will work both openly and covertly, seeking everywhere to co-operate with individuals and groups in undermining American interests and bringing her into disrepute through factual revelation and ridicule, but always working within the law; maintaining critical standards in good taste; and standing by the verifiable principles of objective truth.

5 – Amongst other activities the association will publish tracts and leaflets; organise marches and demonstrations and the picketing of American franchises and other corporate business outlets;[34] lobby politicians for their support; fight for the withdrawal of US bases and military hardware; initiate legislation for the seizure or nationalisation of American assets, irrespective of whether they belong to giant corporations or smaller groups; limit the power of American media moguls by

---

[34] No steps should be taken to oppose the activities of independent American enterprises, which should be allowed equal rights with those of any other country.

whatever means; enforce the closure of American fast-food outlets on health grounds; limit the number of films which may be screened in enabling the recovery of national film industries; and re-introduce the corn laws in assisting local agriculture;

XIII – After America: A vision for the future –

1 – Realising the achievement of *Freedom From America International* is meaningless without a vision for a new world order for peace and security.

2 – America has long had contempt for international law and most specifically for the United Nations (refusing to pay her dues to the association for many years), and these factors starkly reflect her unfitness to stand as an honourable member amongst the world family of nations.

3 – *Freedom From America International* looks forward to re-establishing the United Nations as a body of equals exerting her collective authority for the prosperity and eternal peace of the world.

4 – Two choices face the world today: either domination by a barbarous bully with little respect for any people beyond her borders; or consensus amongst the nations of the civilised world based on the rationality of the Kantian ideal for a better future for all.

5 – Most economic ills and political turmoil in the world today are ultimately traceable to the chicanery of the American dollar; and all such problems are only resolvable through returning autonomy to independent peoples under the protective umbrella of an international parliament of mutually respecting nations.

Why it is apt that the International office of *Freedom From America* should be based in Britain and that its founders should be of British nationality

There are several significant reasons as to why the HQ of *Freedom From America International* should be based in Britain and that its founders be British.

Firstly, our closeness to America as a longstanding so-called "Atlantic partner," exposes us to the suspicion of our closest allies as being "bad Europeans," and to the rest of the world as "poodles" only too happy to lick the hands of the great bully, even when it empties our own exchequer and undermines our material well-being. Hence steps must be taken to reverse such compromising impressions.

Secondly, our actual involvement as aggressors in the Iraqi War, against a people who never intended us harm, necessitates that we seek to morally extricate ourselves from the shameful episode. The British people must make more than a gesture! They must stand at the forefront in the struggle against the world bully, in demonstrating they are above the subjectivity of prejudicially favouring their so-called "cousins" across the water.

Thirdly, a country perceived as closer to the USA in terms of traditional alliances and industrial development is clearly better placed in attracting an all-world movement critical of American domination, than a people with a more obvious "chip on its shoulder" against the great bully, for the latter might only succeed in its appeal to countries similarly placed to itself. That is, Britain has greater credibility as a more disinterested party in launching and pursuing effectively a widespread campaign against America than most other countries.

And finally, Britain as the "mother country," cannot be entirely exculpated from blame for responsibility in giving birth to America in the first place, and of course, it is always a parent who should make the first move in admonishing a recalcitrant child.

ARENA BOOKS
Recent publications -
Specialised Academic titles –

Local Democracy in Modern Mexico a study in participatory methods, by **Arturo Flores**
ISBN 0-9543161-3-4
pp. x/295 Notes, Appendices, Illustrations, Index. Dewey classification: 352.1'4'0972
Retail price: £25.00

Globalisation & Manufacturing Decline aspects of British industry, by **Nicola R. Hothi**
ISBN 0-9543161-4-2
pp. xiv/197 Notes, Appendices, Illustrations. Dewey classification: 338.4'7'629222'0942496
Retail price: £25.00

Political Science titles -

Freedom From America for safeguarding democracy & the economic & cultural integrity of peoples, by **Robert Corfe**   ISBN 0-9543161-5-0
pp. xix/222 Notes, Appendices, Index. Dewey classification: 973.9'3
Retail price: £14.99

Robert Corfe's *tetralogy on the theory and practice of Social Capitalism:-*

The Spirit of New Socialism and the end of class-based politics ISBN 0-9543161-2-6
pp. xvii/359 Notes, Appendices, Bibliography, Index. Dewey classification: 320.5'31'0941
Retail price: £16.99

Reinventing Democratic Socialism for People Prosperity   ISBN 0-9538460-0-8
pp. xix/369 Notes, Appendices, Bibliography, Index. Dewey classification: 320.5'315
Retail price: £16.99
(The original grey cover impression of this book is still available @ £12.99 whilst stocks last.)

New Socialist Business Values for Industrial Resurgence   ISBN 0-9538460-4.0
pp. xxi/387 Notes, Appendices, Bibliography, Indices. Dewey classification: 338
Retail price: £17.99

Foundations of New Socialism a vision for the third millennium ISBN 0-9538460-2-4
pp. xvii/260 Notes, Bibliography, Index. Dewey classification: 320.5'315
Retail price: £14.99

Mass market titles -

Our Swindling Finance Houses their exploitation of the vulnerable, by **Guy Tallice**
ISBN 0-9538460-5-9
pp. xxi/121 Dewey classification: 332.1'0941 Retail price: £12.99

Death in Riyadh dark secrets in hidden Arabia, by **Geoff Carter** ISBN 0-9538460-1-6
pp. 230 Dewey classification: 915.3'80453   Retail price: £14.99

My Conflict With A Soviet Spy the story of the Ron Evans spy case, by **Eddie Miller**
ISBN 0-9538460-3-2
pp. xv/261 Illustrations Dewey classification: 327.1'2'092
Retail price: £14.99